Natalya Carrier

Unconventional truth about learning engagement in tech

AF210173

Natalya Carrier

Unconventional truth about learning engagement in tech

How tech people find fulfillment in companies committed to learning, sharing, purpose and resilience.

Impressum

Bibliografische Information der Deutschen Nationalbibliothek:
Die Deutsche Nationalbibliothek verzeichnet diese
Publikation in der Deutschen Nationalbibliografie; detaillierte
bibliografische Daten sind im Internet über http://dnb.dnb.de
abrufbar.

Verlag: BoD · Books on Demand GmbH, In de Tarpen 42,
22848 Norderstedt, bod@bod.de

Druck: Libri Plureos GmbH, Friedensallee 273, 22763
Hamburg

ISBN: 978-3-7693-0751-1

Nineteen years working in learning and development endowed me with an unexpected heritage. Working amid advanced solutions and the techy people creating them, I was in need to find a new professional aspiration. One by one, art, traveling and coaching came to my life to help me with new senses.

My trips and visits to museums made me increasingly curious of human evolution through learning, history, and its impact on our society. With coaching, I came to understand the power of transformative questions in leading people to exploring new perspectives of their lives. All this, through years, fueled my inner passion for discovering learning cultures inside companies, human mindsets and an understanding of the core values that stand behind our learning and sharing.

From organizing professional communities to holding contests, from working with company universities to running international educational programs, every project looked unique to me. Being lucky enough to organize and at the same time participate in hundreds of training programs, I learnt from everyone, watching participants and keeping my head focused on their learning values. As it looked, there was nothing common I could use as a reference in my next project. I began questioning myself:

- Are all tech people driven by the same value of achievement and recognition?
- Do we all see a pay rise or career promotion as a learning outcome?
- Why do some of us continuously learn and share their knowledge?
- How are learning and our dreams connected?

This questioning grew into a deeper discovery of learning values.

Every new company I joined, I found the same patterns repeated: in the organizational culture, business challenges and people management. Tech people often seek fulfillment beyond their work routine. Most of them are not enough to just complete the same tasks day-by-day. They need meaningful projects where they can grow in their roles and as individuals. There is something in the company atmosphere that inspires them to engage as learners, mentors, authors, and experts, sharing ideas, designing content and transforming themselves and others around.

Various statistics say, we typically spend about one-third of our lives working. If we believe in this, it becomes clear why work is often a source where we seek meaning and senses beyond just money-making or a new title.

It happens, when outside our workspace we undertake new learning impressed by a trainer's personality or a novelty of the topic. Upon finishing that learning, we could not immediately realize the long-term effect it may have on our future. Years later we could remember that very one course or a speech that launched a chain of our greatest life changes. Seems like a hidden magic was at play.

I have collected stories from my tech work and life experience, from talking to other people, from reading and noticing. Some details have been changed to protect other people's privacy and my own sensitive information.

If you work alongside others or lead people in tech or any other domain, you will find inspiration in ideas and a deeper understanding of why people around you learn and share. And what is special in a company atmosphere that influences business and individual transformations.

Maybe you are the one who stays long in one organization or have already changed many workplaces, and now in search of fulfillment. Then this book is here to spark your mind and guide you to find your purpose or a mission with the help of learning and sharing.

CHAPTER 1

LEARNING CULTURE

*There are only three measurements that tell you nearly everything
you need to know about your organization's overall performance:
employee engagement, customer satisfaction, and cash flow.*

Jack Welch, Ex-CEO General Electric

Learning comes to our life on the first day of our life adventure. We start looking around, driven by our curiosity to see how this world works. We master the art of walking, exploring food tastes, new toys, and practicing with words. We observe the habits and beliefs of our parents, siblings and surroundings. By mirroring them, we learn from their experience. Home with its residents and guests is the first place teaching us how to learn.

More complex things open up to us at school where everything is adapted for the learning process: classes with desks and teachers, libraries with books, and of course, teaching content measured by grades. We do homework, take exams, and talk about our school life with parents and friends. Schools together with teachers build the foundation of our learning mindsets.

In college or university, if it happens to us, we prepare for our future jobs. Again surrounded by teachers, books and grades, we obtain new skills to become successful in this world. After graduation, we begin our corporate life in a place made for generating money. It awaits us to implement our learning into something more or less tangible and profitable, like products and services. Our first employer is where we meet corporate and learning cultures as they are. And very often, the way they work in the organization either supports our growth and skill development or destroys our motivation.

My first job interview in IT happened in 2006 when I was still an undergraduate. A young lady walked me through the endless corridors to get to my future boss's room for a talk. To reduce my stress and hopefully feed my brain with dopamine, I was looking around. This corridor brought an interesting observation. A guy wearing home sleepers grabbed a cup from his table, and smiled at me. I followed him to the kitchen, listening to his sleepers rustling on the soft carpet. What can I say, carpets were everywhere, including in the small kitchen area full of people talking and drinking coffee that he turned into. I will remember this place for its mix of smells, freshly made coffee and fitted carpets.

The corridors were decorated with photos in wooden frames. As I found out later, this local hall of fame aimed to emphasize winners of the yearly photo contest. It was a big honor for everyone to participate and get this recognition. Next to the boss's room was a big company logo and several certificates, among them a Microsoft certificate. I was even more drawn to the end of the corridor with shelves full of books and magazines anyone could take for free, as I was later told in my interview.

Many years have passed, but I still remember all those details. It was my first introduction to organizational culture, of which I knew nothing. All the little things, the logo and photos, a guy in home sleepers, the people in the kitchen, all that highlighted to me: I am in the right place. And it really turned out as I had expected. What I saw on the way to that interview grew into bigger and more valuable findings later.

Several years after that interview, the time came to change the direction of my career path. Not that I was an initiator of that. Rather the world crisis initiated that for me. Four months after

I had quit, I was invited back to join the same company in a new role delivering training projects. After that offer, I learned what the impostor syndrome is. I kept thinking of my zero knowledge and complete incompetence in training. But my curiosity and willingness to learn won the battle. I made myself see a similarity between training and the event management I had done during an earlier public relations career. And that helped me to overcome my uncertainty.

Much later I realized that my puzzle was finally complete. All I wanted to do was promote learning. My marketing background turned my new job into an exciting journey. Every project I did got me closer to understanding why we learn, share and what really engages us to do that.

Very soon my brain helped me with that search. I discovered the Iceberg model introduced by Edward T. Hall, an American anthropologist and author of the book Beyond the Culture (1976). This model became my inspiration to look deeper and find the place of a learning culture hidden somewhere on both sides of the waterline. All elements of the initial model indicate to me their direct or indirect relation to learning. It is true to say that a learning culture is not a single culture in an organization. It stands next to different other elements, like ethics and inclusivity, transformation, leadership, customer-centric approach and probably more. In this book I will only explore the learning cultures in which I have the biggest interest.

A learning culture is one of the components of an organizational culture. It determines practices, approaches, models, behaviors, values and beliefs related to learning, knowledge sharing and personnel development. Company leaders are those who initiate, develop and bring learning cultures to the end.

At the first glance, a concept of a learning culture, with its practices and approaches, sounds very academic. However, within a company, it is a totally business project, as many call it not much learning, but rather performance culture. It requires financial and human investments, a certain plan and drivers to implement and bring expected results to life. My experience with numerous learning projects is set in this model. It highlights obvious (or public) and hidden (internal) parts of the learning cultures I was happy to observe and build.

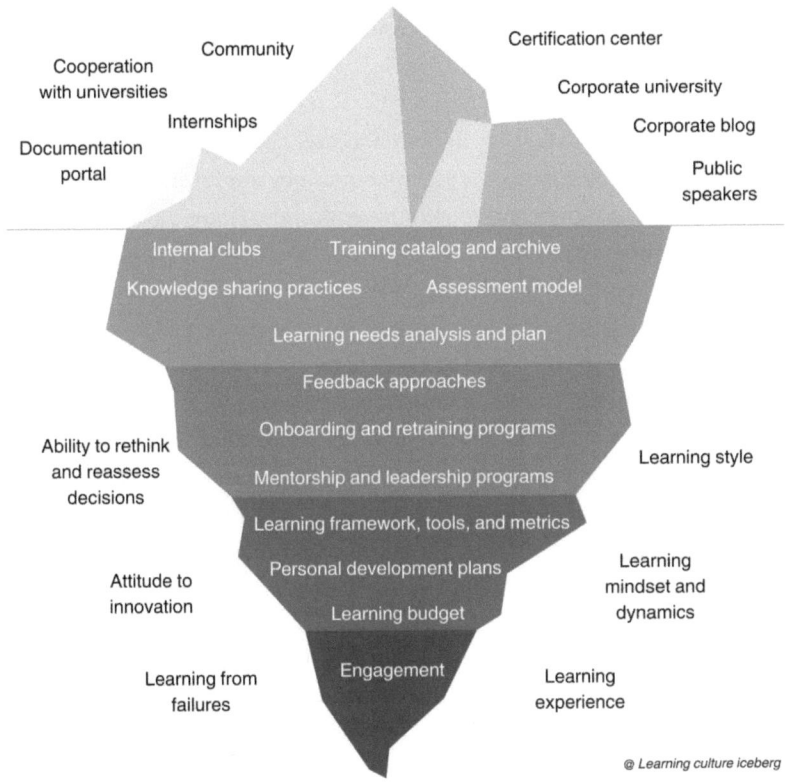

Cooperation
with universities

Community

Certification center

Corporate university

Internships

Documentation
portal

Corporate blog

Public
speakers

Internal clubs · Training catalog and archive

Knowledge sharing practices · Assessment model

Learning needs analysis and plan

Feedback approaches

Onboarding and retraining programs

Ability to rethink
and reassess
decisions

Mentorship and leadership programs

Learning style

Learning framework, tools, and metrics

Personal development plans

Attitude to
innovation

Learning budget

Learning
mindset and
dynamics

Engagement

Learning from
failures

Learning
experience

@ Learning culture iceberg

What does it all look like in real life?

When I need to check any footprint of a learning culture, I go
with corporate social media and websites. The first thing that
usually attracts my attention is the *Who we are* and *What we do*
sections, which you will find in roughly ninety percent of

company websites. Sometimes written as text, sometimes hidden between the lines, companies manifest learning in their corporate values.

My investigation continues on a career page. Along with vacancies, it may offer internships. They aim to attract the brightest applicants to join the upskill programs.
A career page may overview assessment services. Being a standalone entity or one of the corporate university services, it signals learning culture elements. For instance, product tech companies I have seen usually have documentation portals to share public guides, manuals, and how-to's with their end-users. I have seen these implemented as independent platforms or public repositories with easy access, like Git. How else do companies spread a word on their learning initiatives? Sometimes I notice learning related articles on corporate blogs. Among those there might be news on cooperation with educational institutions. These joint projects pursue the idea to reduce the gap between institutional programs and business expectations, help young scientists with finding a base for their discoveries, test scientific hypotheses, and a lot more.

Yet another example from tech companies is to have public communities. Aiming to involve partners and customers into various company initiatives, community platforms gather continuous feedback on the company product or services, support its members in a peer-to-peer format, and of course, enhance the brand position on the market. As communities are unique structures, it is almost impossible to make a complete copy of any community and achieve the same results with the same functions.

All these elements may indicate a presence of a learning culture in the company.

If nothing is found in public sources, does it mean that a company ignores learning needs? It could be the case. Or, a company may want to keep it private.

Here comes another perspective at what usually happens inside the company.

Imagine an ideal technology enterprise with a broad learning culture. A young manager, we call her Ashley, wants to join the company and lead a team of ten people. This is how Ashley observes the presence of a learning culture.

1.   Interview phase

During the interview process, a recruiter emphasizes the company's values, particularly its commitment to fostering continuous development across the company. Ashley discusses with interviewers her openness to fast learning, prompted by questions about acquiring new skills, committing to continuous learning, and staying updated with industry and project management trends.

2.   Probation period

Once her journey in the company begins, she starts working according to the onboarding training plan with a dedicated mentor. The personalized onboarding plan suggests a list of self-paced courses, real-life scenarios, video recordings, series of templates, and other learning materials based on Ashley's background and her role in the company.

Her mentor provides her with continuous feedback on regular check-up calls. Based on this and other peers' feedback, Ashley can see her patterns, strengths and areas for improvement.

Ashley has her first big performance review at the end of her probation period. The aim of that meeting is to summarize her biggest achievements, give detailed feedback from stakeholders and define next steps. From that process, she learns about the model People and Culture or HR team uses to evaluate employees' performance and create learning plans. Her company works with a 360-degree model that also implies personal development plans to support employees in achieving their goals within a time frame.

3.   Employment phase

A personalized development plan becomes a valuable source for Ashley to continue her professional development within the company as an employee. It includes key areas for her growth, ways of implementing new skills and obtaining new knowledge, important deadlines, etc. The plan is easy to access and track changes. Ashley works on her development plan with her manager and a mentor rolled into one.

Being in a manager role requires Ashley to organize and conduct one-on-one meetings with her team members. The HR department has already articulated a recommended approach in communicating progress and performance at such meetings with employees. Ashley learns that constructive type of feedback is highly welcomed in the company.

3.1 First year assessment

In a year, Ashey will undergo her first major assessment. According to the company rules, all employees have to go through that process once or twice per year.

3.2 Next employment phase

Learning planning

In big enterprises with dedicated learning functions, planning usually starts with the learning needs analysis. It can take place as an anonymous survey, by interviewing leadership or entire teams, and with the help of AI tools. This analysis and historical data turn into a learning plan with all activities to be held within a year. Ashley actively contributes ideas to the plan. She is excited to make her team and her company as a whole even more productive next year. A set of quantitative metrics complements a learning plan to assess outcomes at the end of a year. These metrics may include a number of certified people per year, levels of learners' engagement, top ten most viewed e-learning courses, and many others. Ashley has access to the real-time data. She can easily find training reports to follow her team's performance and see how they engage with training resources on the company platform.

Learning budget

A learning plan becomes a source of reference for a learning budget to support expenses on attending conferences, supporting internal clubs, managing certifications, and hosting a video archive. Tools for content authoring, online proctoring, mindmapping, and learning subscriptions (for example, management of podcast subscriptions, e-book subscriptions, vouchers on software, etc.) are a part of the budget too. The company learning culture thrives on its broad integration of artificial intelligence technologies and a collaborative employee-driven approach.

Continuous learning

As a manager, Ashley knows how to apply for a conference herself, request it for her team members, and justify new software installation for continuous growth.

On her way, Ashley meets various team's use cases where learning is necessary. For instance, one of her team members decides to go through retraining. It is to enhance their skills necessary for a job change within the company. Another one figures out how to grow as a mentor and future leader in Ashley's team. For that, the company offers a set of mentorship and leadership programs to assist in the employee learning goals.

Community and sharing knowledge

Ashley plays a crucial role in the company's leadership club. She moderates club meetings and actively manages the club agenda while others share their projects' learning experience and best practices at the quarterly leadership events.

All company employees know where to search for learning opportunities, who is in charge of helping them, and the process of getting approval is pretty clear. Learning experience is not just on paper, it is live, continuous and worthwhile. Employees have an easy-to-search and navigate learning management platform customized to their needs. They can easily book seats, participate in online workshops and access bite-sized lessons delivered weekly that are tailored to their learning habits and progress.The catalog of learning materials keeps growing over time. The company's learning mindset promotes success and continuous improvement.

Ashley's team members are actively involved in knowledge sharing practices between departments, teams and individuals. The company supports employees in discussing project failures and lessons learnt during knowledge sharing sessions.

The choice of words, the tone of voice used to give feedback, mentor others, and present information define the learning style set in the company. Ashley is preparing to speak at the next company conference. She is thrilled to become a speaker and this way promotes learning as a company value.

This is a very brief overview with no end.

In this model, learners' and leadership engagement outshine other elements. In many cases I observed, it is one or both of them that turn other elements of the learning culture on. When I say *learner engagement*, I refer to the value-driven involvement, meaning that each learner has a sense of motivation to participate in the learning process for themselves or contribute to other people's learning. And that differs it from employee engagement, which is a broader term. I define it to myself as a mix of caring attitude and supportive behavior of an employee that builds a foundation for loyalty and commitment within a company. It is true, like many observe, that engagement is not only a part of a company's life. It stays with us in our lives no matter what our employment is.

Similar to learner engagement, leadership engagement is based on seeing a true business value of supporting learning initiatives across the company.

Here are several examples to illustrate it better.

Imagine a company developing a complicated tech product. No one in the company takes documentation seriously. Leaders and content contributors ignore its importance. The documentation portal looks unstructured and mostly outdated. The outcome for the business and end customers? Without access to the up-to-date materials on the portal, customers may decide to leave the company, unhappy about losing time and money on self-learning. A potential loss for the company.

Another example. A big enterprise with a complicated hierarchy. The onboarding process of new hires is blurred. No one wants to become a mentor as it is not a priority according to the human resource department and line managers. Newbies randomly meet their mentors and seek information themselves. The criteria for completing the onboarding are missing. No engagement on mentors' and leadership sides leads to time and money losses. New hires feel disengaged and stressed.

Does it mean that all companies should have all these elements implemented to become successful? Surely not. It all depends on a company's business needs, its size, budgets, hierarchy, expansion plans and more.

I have observed a company with a very basic learning culture, where the entire learning process for newbies going through their probation only meant being mentored by seniors. A bunch of articles helped newbies with the technological processes. That's it. Was it enough for this company? For that moment of time, yes.

Have I ever seen an example where the learner engagement level grew with no leadership support? I have not, because in any company leaders are the same learners. If they have teams to manage, their teams' performance directly influences their own metrics. If you want to grow the plant, you have to water it regularly.

Education is the most powerful weapon, which you can use to change the world.

Nelson Mandela

Any learning we do moves us towards a change. Big or small. Immediate or deferred. Expected or surprising. Within or around us. Time and time again I repeat this mantra to myself. The job of selling courses reminded me about it every working day. Do not believe anyone saying that a course is an easy product to sell. It took me, a complete newbie in sales, quite an extra effort.

First, I had to reflect on the idea that a learning course is a non-tangible product that doesn't really exist. It is only digital. And I want people to buy it for money. And that will require them to struggle and sometimes sweat. They will breathe indoors, at a desk or in front of a camera, while they could be enjoying a lovely weekend time with their families and friends outdoors. Second, I want them to pay, struggle, and be separated from their families for two or more days that should transform their lives after. Which actually means yet another challenge. And finally, the cherry on top: this course might be one out of dozens a person needs to take to achieve their goal. So, learning expenses might only grow. Too much for a course, isn't it? This experience pushed my discovery of learning values forward.

We should admit that people are emotional and irrational creatures. Even our rationality often falls under our irrationality. When people buy a course and declare that it is for their joy only, there is always a greater need behind that unconscious purchase. When people invest in learning with a great purpose in mind, it can either turn into a significant transformation or fail to materialise.

The more I convinced people to change their lives with my company courses, the more I found how diverse values influence their purchases and actions taken after the course ends. Let me explain what I mean by saying *change*.

A change for a learner may take different formats. They may want within their employing company:

1. A new competence

Competencies are built from specific knowledge, hard and soft skills. Knowing a theory and practice of a particular programming language refers to hard skills. Communication, leadership, and similar skills we consider as soft skills. New competencies enable us to perform new tasks. With competencies, we can influence the quality of our work, make more productive decisions, and expand areas of responsibility. Around fifteen years ago, I heard from technical consultants that soft skills were seen as less important for a career than hard skills. Or they are something only managers need. At that time, a developer's work was commonly seen as full-time coding, testing and working in front of a screen with no interaction and communication with people. It was not at all. Luckily, the situation has changed when numerous trainers and speakers stepped up to address the problem, and soft skills became recognised as crucial for tech people career success.

2.   A new behavior

Theory without practice, as we know, brings no use. While practice through a set of actions turns into a new behavior. Usually, with a specific knowledge our confidence boosts, so that we want to apply it in real projects. And so we start for the first time creating a plan, automating a system, taking ownership of bigger initiatives, or mentoring others within our teams. I remember one senior manager with dozens of managers under her supervision. In her work profile she placed a quote next to her signature that read: *Do not ask for permission, ask for forgiveness*. Every time I used to contact this person via email, I could not ignore the quote, as it was publicly seen for multiple years. Being continuously busy, she used the quote to promote a proactive behavior among her subordinates and others within the company emailing her.

3.   A leveling up

Literally, it is a process of recognition and promotion to a higher position within a company. Usually we associate it with demonstrated competence, ability to take on more responsibilities, showing a hard-working attitude, and willingness to climb the career ladder. The process is strongly related to company processes and policies. In tech enterprises, the process usually lasts several months and requires rounds of communication, including human resource and line managers.

4. A pay raise

In certain companies a pay raise starts with the salary review process, and it goes hand in hand with a career promotion. Sometimes a pay raise does not happen along with a level-up. It may sound evident that when a role extends with new tasks, it should correlate with the salary. But it is not always so. Some people are absolutely fine with having a title, like Chief Officer of something, with no salary raise. In such cases, money is not the biggest value. The title matters most. For companies with a particular company culture it might be normal to give a new title without investing into a salary raise. Opposite to the case above, we should understand that there are people who will be fine with learning something continuously, taking more responsibilities without any pompous titles and promotions. As long as it pays super well, they stay engaged.

5. Learning as a value

It does not really matter how we name this value, would it be learning, education, self-development, growth or self-advancement, but it can be something we have carried with us since our school or university. It could also be developed in adulthood as we – begin noticing the outcomes of our efforts with our first, second and next promotion or a salary raise. When we see others achieving more through learning and sharing, their examples inspire us to make learning our habit and life value.

6. New environment and contacts

Most tech people I have observed want to be among other smart and enthusiastic people to continuously deliver things together, learn from their experience and get inspired. A tech community is diverse with a wide range of different characters. Among those, you can find lots of people who could define them as *introverted*. And being long among others for some of them sounds, politely speaking, uncomfortable. New environments, like a company community or a Meetup gathering, where all people look similar style, become a safe and comfortable place for sharing diverse opinions and ideas. Open communication, along with a cozy environment, allows techy people to see a sense in personal fulfillment and chitchat benefits. That stimulates curiosity that leads to better decisions.

When examining change from an individual perspective and a broader scale, we may identify that we also strive for:

1. A new identity

We have already mentioned a level-up in the company, when someone earns a new title. Here we will look at it from a broader perspective. Like a specific role or self-identity that requires knowledge, skills, competencies and self-development practices mastered and accumulated over years. For instance, to become a project manager, one should work on communication, problem-solving, leadership, time management and other skills along with technical knowledge and domain expertise.

Becoming a director in the company, a freshly made entrepreneur, inventor of a new technique, professional podcaster and so on describes our new identities and requires a unique set of skills and abilities. All depends on how big we want to grow, and what is the scale of our dreams and identities. As you may find, the identity answers the question: *Who am I*, which sounds too philosophic. If you try this question or similar: *Who we are now and who we want to be next?* on yourself and your close circle, you will see how hard it is for many of us to give a certain answer.

2.   Long-term opportunities

A good example of this may be a new country for living and working. A new lifestyle with a set of habits, or any new horizon that attracts a person. Learning new languages is one of my favorite examples to illustrate this type of change. When someone becomes proficient with a new language to get ready for the upcoming studies and work abroad. Learning a new language may speed up our adaptation process when we decide to settle in a new country and find a new place to name 'home'. Learning a new language opens for us new doors to international communities, resources like books, reports, etc. And finally, a new language we have learned brings us closer to understanding who we are (see the point above).

3.   Finding the mission

The second philosophical question we can explore through learning is: *What is the mission of my life?* Both personal experiences and the passage of time trigger us to ask this question and seek an answer. From my observation, throughout our lives, learning and sharing can bring us closer to our truths.

Our employing company can become that place where we fulfill our life missions. At the same time, we as employees, can use a company's resources and support to discover our missions outside our work: in different hobbies, pet-projects we do on weekends, in family and friends time together. All that becomes possible in companies where personal development values as much as professional.

These are the big reasons we jump into learning to make a conscious change. But it is not that simple. Later we will unpack the layers of learning values and beliefs to see our true nature.

What kind of change does a company expect from its employees taking any learning?
Many companies declare that learning is their key value to enhance employee performance and thus increase productivity. We may also see that companies want employees to learn to make better business decisions. For this, companies invest in leadership and managerial programs and grow talents across all levels. A strong team with collective intelligence keeps retention rates high, and the company's brand strong on the market.

All these reasons should be considered through the prism of revenue and business profit, which are the main goal of any business. Learning is not an exception. All training initiatives should always be aligned with the business goals. Let us open cards to see the business side of these statements.

Look at employee performance, and you will find its influence on production and sales. The more and with better quality a company produces within a time frame, the more they can offer and sell to customers. Better quality products lead to a higher number of satisfied customers and their loyalty in generating long-term profit for the company.

A skilled and integrated team of leaders brings the company to the top. They are key drivers of the collective intelligence to emerge. They influence employees' performance across the organization. Then grown up talents move from the bottom to the upper level of the hierarchy and are able to implement creative solutions that can generate more revenue for the company.

More engaged and satisfied employees help a company to keep key people on board, spending less money on continuous recruiting and filling role gaps in the production process. And, as we discovered above, when an employee reaches a level-up, increases financial expectations and develops new habits in the new environment, the company becomes an attractive place to work and talk about. It gives the company an obvious competitive advantage and ability to face any uncertainties with strength and potential.

When I only started my work on this book, I focused my narration on the pure function of learning. As I would go to explain things, like learning engagement and learning culture across everywhere. And then I wondered, where is the place for sharing? It must be here.

Learning and sharing are linked processes. For every learner, there is a sharer. In the learner role, we accumulate knowledge and skills, giving new energy to our dreams and wishes. On the way, mentors, trainers, book authors, video bloggers, friends, and peers become our sharers. They walk next to us to help with our change. At some point, we become ready to participate in building collective intelligence. We speak in public, write, document, talk to peers, mentor interns, and thus we foster collaboration and recreate new ideas and insights around us. This is the story when others become our learners, directly or indirectly.

So, what drives our learning and sharing? Curiosity does. And here I totally support Todd Kashdan, professor of psychology. According to him, one of the dimensions of curiosity is a joyful exploration: *the recognition and desire to seek out new knowledge and information and a subsequent joy of learning and growing.*

Take another look at the definition to grasp its depth and fullness. It contains one of the key values that drives our learning and sharing – being recognised. It explains our desire as an internal motive to start the process. It talks about joy, which matters much to keep our interest high. And it emphasizes growing, confirming our actions towards better change in us.

Above we have identified what kind of changes we await. It can look to us as a career promotion or a level-up. It may bring us recognition through a pay raise. We can find a new identity for ourselves. We can seek long-term opportunities. And, we may want more contacts and a new environment for us.

But if that is the case, this book should end on the next page. Wait a bit. I am here to give you some ideas I have learnt and observed in many years. In the next chapters you will find my personal vision on learning and sharing values supported with different stories. I want you to look at these linked processes from another angle, like, our willingness to leave a footprint. Or becoming a part of learning and sharing projects driven by empathy and social responsibility. For that, we may pick one or another format of learning and sharing because we need to escape and to hedge our bets. You will find examples of self-learning and group learning. You will find stories that happened because of a strong learning culture and driven by self-motivation only.

CHAPTER 2

LEGACY AND IMPACT

When we hear the word *legacy*, our immediate association could take us back to the past with its traditions and history of sharing wisdom from one generation to the next. We could also associate *legacy* with life's imprints, when someone leaves behind a contribution to be remembered once gone. In the tech world, legacy not only carries the qualities from the above but also has its own meaning.

During my work for big tech enterprises, I observed young and enthusiastic developers expressing their preferences to pioneering projects and new technologies. Being hired for a long-term project usually meant, according to the rumor, to work with outdated systems. All because of complex legacy systems with countless code lines, written by other developers earlier, that are difficult to read and maintain, they said. In the world of technology, where everything has a tendency to be fast and creative, legacy projects look unattractive for those who want to build a system from scratch and leave a fingerprint. I have heard people justifying their choices, often starting with a question: *Why would I even participate in something old-looking, knowing that numerous startups await me?* But let us be honest, only a few of us are born to create a new software development framework, a pearl of wisdom or a new energy source technology. A book, article, podcast series, app or painting will satisfy many of us. We are pretty fine if our contribution will be seen as somehow remarkable but smaller.

I have also seen legacy in the companies where top people, unique competency holders, or so-called stars, used to leave the company or shift to another department. The reason for quitting or shifting does not really matter here. The question is in the situation, where these people left when unable to contribute their input.

Another situation where legacy matters is the case with the same stars or knowledge keepers who already spent many years with a single company but lost motivation. It happens to them sporadically. And for yet another case, to keep the stars on track, the company managers invent a project where skills and competencies of such people are crucial. It can be a corporate university initiative, launch of group internships from scratch, setup of a new automated system, creation of product documentation, and many more.

Explore the story of a company that recently decided to start training for the public. They found Ben, a skilled person in-house, to deliver content for customers onsite. New to training and content development but with a strong expertise in the company domain, he took on the project, learning and adapting as he went.

For several years, live workshops ran smoothly. Learners were engaged in the process of learning and felt empowered with the company services. Along with the growing level of customer satisfaction, the initiative brought money back to the company, compensating all expenses of the trainer's travels and workshop delivery.

The challenge came once Ben decided to quit. After some checks, managers found very few artifacts left by Ben. There was a single presentation with slides and some graphics, but zero notes. It happened so because no one ever questioned him what was going on behind the scenes.
As it usually happens, Ben's departure from the company became the talk of the office. Everyone wondered who would handle these tasks after he was off. No one in the company was considering a trainer's position as an attractive place to apply immediately. Customers were knocking the door as they still wanted to buy the workshop. Here is what the company decided.

They announced one of the conditions under which Ben could leave the company. It was to create an e-learning course out of the presentation and slides he had used in the workshop. The company involved a camera guy who helped with the video production. They were fine with using the existing materials. With one exception, practical exercises had to be explained in a step-by-step manner to help learners progress on their paths. The project took about two weeks of intense work.

After the job was done, the company was benefiting from the ready-made e-learning for several years. Even when the new trainer came to replace Ben in his role as a workshop trainer, no one could make the course better than he had. The number of views and reviews was so remarkable that every time the question of postponing any maintenance of this course turned into a series of long discussions. Ben was a perfect match not only for the onsite course, but for e-learning too. His tone of voice, his presence on the video, the expert look, the depth and simplicity of explanations, and the quality of exercises were above expectations. In several years of active course use, the company was ready to archive and replace it with a freshly made e-learning alternative.

After quitting the job and closing the chapter of being a hired employee, Ben established his own company and began a new story of leaving a legacy to this world with his own software product.

This example of a legacy happened under compelling circumstances related to staff termination. The ideal scenario would be in having every content piece documented with notes for existing and future speakers. And this is what big companies with broad learning cultures usually do. To me, the story confirms how in a short time, a company can produce valuable content and achieve significant results for their end-users allowing their loyal experts to pursue their true calling.

With legacy in the philosophical sense, I still have the question open. Is it something common for people under some age? Does this value appear once we cross a particular age? I see a dependency in age, as none of us is immortal. The older we become, the more we might think of what will be left after we are gone. At the same time, I know people who are extremely motivated by their footprint at a young age. Maybe it is a matter of generations, maybe it is a more individual thing. Let us wait and see how the next generation will act.

In her early fifties Maria aspired to pursue a career in entrepreneurship. Her husband saw big risks in stepping into this project, being fully busy with new business and having only a few hours at home. Maria was working on small-size projects for her pleasure and money security and dreaming of building a web studio in her town. In a studio she wanted to see people from her home place to support the local community she had strong roots with after her immigration. After several attempts to make a deep dive into business, Maria and her husband agreed on her continuing working for the enterprise as a hired project manager. This way this job brought more security and comfort to their relationship and the future of their kids.

At some point, Maria discovered herself in a new role – a content author. Her company was actively recruiting people to become voices of the product they developed. For that, they wanted managers and tech leaders to speak at public events and create content for sharing on different online platforms. The management offered complete support for trainers, hiring public speaking trainers and creating several online courses to enable the project members.

Maria found this idea fascinating and happily joined the project. She unlocked her own style and method to produce easy-to-understand video lessons and explain technology concepts of the company product and services. She used her native language and a few others to create multi-language content for one of the world-known course-hosting platforms. Many friends were curious about the video production process and her author income. She preferred to avoid answering. But from the sparkles in her eyes, they could guess about the joy and monetary satisfaction the project brought her.

When someone asked her opinion on the topics people like asking on the platform, she stayed open in sharing her insights. It became evident that any topic might attract commercial learners. Maria started recording a video series about her management style, getting a visa permit to work abroad and learning multiple languages in the fastest way. All that allowed her to become an independent author and trainer.

From time to time, Maria heard the voice of her motherland calling for her business to manifest its social duty. It became stronger every time she reflected on her childhood poverty and limited opportunities for her family and classmates to achieve something greater in the low-developed country. She considered herself lucky and blessed to be able to study abroad and get monthly income hundreds times higher than her classmates could only get working hard in her mother town for years. Every time she felt upset by putting aside the idea of building a company and supporting her compatriots with something meaningful. However, the project she did for the company and later for herself as a content author made her feel proud of the impact she could bring to someone's lives and be remembered after. After a while, she considered the project an opportunity to become a content entrepreneur.

Working for a company gives us many opportunities to leave our mark. In Maria's case, her company with a broad learning culture allowed her to unlock the best of skills and even combine her own projects with the company's initiatives. The content platforms served her to keep a record of projects and leave legacy in the fast-changing IT environment. This story is about getting passive income to support oneself on retirement or a sublimation of an entrepreneurship role. It makes sense here too.

If you are a hired employee with a strong need for leaving legacy and impact, search for such projects in-house to fulfill your values. As a manager, look around, and you will recognise people's talents to make a change. Perhaps, you have your child dreams that are still sleeping? Look inside and maybe you will find the answers to your legacy drive.

I met people who were much bigger than their current jobs and titles, already prepared to accomplish their life missions, but who chose to set boundaries and wait. I also met those who dreamed smaller than they are, limiting their potential. Luckily, learning has the power to break the limits we create in our minds.

MARTA

Since childhood Marta has dreamed of becoming an artist. At her little five, she started sketching famous fairy tales. Not that she was practicing with a notepad, getting ready for her first school year, but rather experimenting with reinventing well-known stories like, Rapunzel and Sleeping Beauty. She practiced with changing the characters' family places, adding antagonists and new details. For her when a child, painting was a tool for inventing her own world where she felt herself to the full. To support her passion, she added written stories. They are still somewhere at her grandparents' place, together with her illustrations.

Marta's first public exhibition happened at her ten. At home, for her parents, everything went well. But not this time, at a typical school day event, where all kids from her class were involved in the exhibition activities. There were mosaics, clay figures, painted boxes, and her black-and-white art selected by her teacher who enthusiastically supported her with a first presentation. She felt from the start, her painting stood out of the crowd.

Waiting silently at the back of the exhibition hall, she caught herself thinking about how far she was from competing with 3D-printed fantasy characters, wooden toys and hand-made T-shirts. Full of colors and small details, they immediately drew all eyes on them and gathered a crowd around, while her art attracted random passersby.

She imagined her first exhibition full of admired feedback. Instead, she heard her classmates whispering: *These works are so boring*. All these comments hit her hard as she spent hours preparing something special for this day. In thirty minutes she found herself leaving the main hall.

Full of tears, standing by the door, she hardly tried to wipe them off her face. Her teacher tried to bring her back to the room. In fifteen minutes she was ready for the party to continue. Burying it deep within, she never truly forgot about the episode that almost ruined her interest.

The dream grew up and transformed into a new one, where she works for a magazine as a designer. This job, she imagined, would inspire her with novelty every day. She thought of it as a drive and intrigue of meeting new people with their stories, from which she can learn the meaning of life. Of course, she dreamt of becoming a part of some nation-scale team, where her designer role was crucial for the story's success. But it did not happen this way.

In her adulthood, this dream kept going. Marta created a profile under a fake name on platforms for artists. She trained her skills and used it for feedback. It worked for her. But she could take from it nothing more. During this period, she was surrounded by dozens of people who were pretty good in design. To keep her dream sleeping, she came up with the idea of helping other artists' dreams to come true. This period was full of new learning for her. As she acted as a trainer for young art creators. Through their success, she took a shadow role which was never fed enough. In her spare time, she was part of various online and onsite art programs, truly believing in their after-effects. Where it started, it ended. Seemed like nothing was moving her forward.

Time flew by, and her dream turned into a career in tech companies. First, as a graphic designer and later as content creator. She found a big joy in analyzing data, structuring plans, creating visuals and looking at how learners consume it, thankful for her dedication. The problem with this joy emerged when she faced her first course maintenance. And then the next one, even bigger. Every month she polished a growing catalog with content, as by this moment it had already become outdated. Not just a single course, but the entire catalog. It was her biggest finding: in tech companies and in any fast-changing field, this thing is common for content designers. Unfortunately, there was no chance to automate course maintenance without putting her hands to it. Her joy of publishing a new course turned into an expectation of an upcoming maintenance. Which meant more work to do. And more stress. Her feeling of legacy, how she expected it to be, as a long-lasting benefit for the audience with her standing behind, disappeared. Maybe not completely, but she sensed how a feeling of joy had changed.

Many times she had heard from technical writers responsible for product documentation that they feel the same. Their world turns to a nightmare if the documentation portal has no structure and maintenance process automation. Thousands of articles may become useless overnight once a new product release happens. They face complaints and negative feedback, and their routine becomes harder and harder to manage. Maintenance is not only a thing for people creating content, but also for those who need to rethink new concepts, retrain themselves and implement these changes. Most times in the fastest way possible. And this is how Marta moved forward with her dream. She looked at it from the perspective of the footprint we all want to leave in this life. Should it be a painting, a family cooking book with recipes, a technological invention, an act of kindness spread on by word-of-mouth, a how-to video, a course people use and value, or a fiction book.

Marta's dream of becoming a designer became a confirmation of her other need that was behind. While the content for the tech industry left her no chance to feel the joy to the fullest, she questioned herself: How can I leave a meaningful footprint? How can I be remembered for my impact? And finally, she gathered the courage to restart her illustrations. That was the beginning of a new story, where she unveiled her art in a solo exhibition. But in an unusual way. With the help of her company manager, Marta took the role of an interior designer. Being first responsible for small projects and later for the entire company office look. From ceiling to floor. From wall colors to LED lamps. She was happy to see her projects scale and introduced to a big public daily.

I do not really believe this is the end of Marta's story. Most likely she is still out there, working with interior projects, while searching for her path to fulfill the dream and take a first step forward. Who knows what is next for her when our future holds endless possibilities.

Working with learning and development functions requires being open to marketing, sales, public relations, legal and operations inquiries. In my experience with big enterprises, I used to allocate a significant amount of time to joint projects with PR specialists. Among various contests and hiring initiatives we did together, social responsibility projects hold a remarkable place. They always bring a company more than an immediate benefit. They are about business responsibility, to keep eyes open and react with actions to society signals and demands.

One of such projects I did together with the public relations team is still in my memory. Five pre-planned days a week we hosted evening workshops in the company venue. Each day we aimed to highlight one of IT-specific areas, like project management, quality assurance, data science and so on. For each event we chose topics that were trendy and important for the company's growth. My work was to find charismatic speakers well or less known in the industry, agree on participation, decide on inspirational topics, and coach them to speak in front of the audience if they had never done it before.

Usually, we had two speakers per evening and around one hundred people in a room. At first two times, then four times per year, we did this event to meet diverse social needs, like helping kids, animal shelters, or ecological communities. The entrance to each evening cost a symbolic sum of money regulated by the company. People were able to donate extra if they wanted to. And many were ready to follow. Later the format moved to online and was a great success for several years in a row.

I felt proud to participate. I knew my effort was not for the company goals only, but rather for those who require unspoken help and attention. I noticed the same response while communicating the project goals to potential speakers. Working for zero payment and being supported with travel expenses only, they easily committed to investing their own time in preparing and delivering their speeches. By my calculation, I got around 10% rejection because of other plans scheduled for the day of the event. None of them said the project went against their employers' interests or they saw no value for them to take part.

Both speakers and attendees described their experience as a commitment to the project with a meaningful purpose. I still remember a conversation I had with Kate. I learned from her that empathy and positive contribution to society are among her values. Every project and company she chose had more dimensions than solely business. Many years ago she found how feelings of sympathy and altruism were getting a victory over her. She was surrounded by people willing to make this world better by bringing more fairness. She did a lot of money raising for her colleagues in need, cooperated with volunteers to support orphans with clothes and presents on holidays. After one such event she discovered it was too much for her inner self. Her energy was getting extremely low.

Slowly she pulled away from charity projects to keep herself strong. The fairness of life her colleagues and volunteers tried to believe in was crushed as an idea. What happens around gives her more certainty of people's differences, where fairness is a complicated concept.

Her family taught her to never give up. And give a hand to those in need. To support this, she can do other kinds of projects where her heart is filled with joy and happiness. And on her way she found many in her employing company and in the tech world. My invitation was one of many she could not ignore. The project was happy to have her as a speaker for several years in a row and in numerous cities.

I will be one among many stating that the number of women clubs, gatherings, specialized courses and conferences is growing with time. In IT, where I accumulated my experience through many years, the topic is still trendy: whether IT is a good place for women to work and grow as technology consultants, leaders, and even company owners. Not strange at all, but there are no similar clubs for men in IT. Have you heard of any? Here is one of the stories how it all works within company learning cultures.

It started at one of the company's internal events, where employees, eighty five percent of which are men, get together to discuss technical novelties and ideas. Usually, one or two people gave short presentations, and the evening ended peacefully with no intense debates. There was not a single case of women performing on stage. Not that there were no topics to share. Low initiative and inconfidence to speak played a role in it, where women acted as listeners who rarely asked questions, preferring to stay out of the spotlight.
This event has never been a place for newbies to learn about the company and its culture. For that they had a week of onboarding initiatives. But this time, someone offered to invite recent hires and finish the event somehow differently than typical pizza, beer and poker. The idea has been met with enthusiasm. Especially by the human resource department who agreed to support the event.

Before it started, current employees anonymously wrote ice-breaking questions on paper and shared with organizers. At the event, according to the plan, all newbies are invited to draw questions from a hat, read them and answer aloud in front of the participants. Organizers believed the activity format would create an atmosphere of honesty and spontaneity in responses. And the entire event would be casual, where people joked a lot and had a great time together.

Jenny, one of the technical leaders, had already settled into the company a long time ago. She was considered as one of the most creative consultants who was invited to give opinions on complex project issues. Although she was never on the stage. And not even because in the evenings she played in an amateuer theater in her neighborhood and already had a presenter experience.

She took her seat in the first row with a glass of coke and several slices of pizza, giving an unspoken message – I belong to this tech community of men. From her pose and mimics, one could recognise how cozy and looking forward to the entire event she was.

Two technical speeches at the beginning went unnoticed. The same can not be said about the icebreaker game with newbies. From the first glance, the questions sounded inconsistent. From – how do you calculate angles of a figure. To – what would you choose in certain circumstances – your job or your mom. It was fun for most people in the community, but not everyone.

Jenny was the center of attention and supported the atmosphere. Her voice was heard frequently commenting on every question and answer. Her and several other men's comments were sarcastic and very close to becoming offensive. The atmosphere shifted beyond just a typical corporate event with its communication standards. Some newbies, among which one you could notice three young women, were left with an unpleasant feeling as their body language showed. They were giving strange smiles to each other. While their faces clearly looked like they were unsure of what had just happened. They never hid their humanitarian self and easily found their place in mixed teams. But this game left them puzzled. Instead of staying with everyone for evening poker, one could see newbies leaving the venue in a hurry when the ice-breaker game was over.

To say the least, the informal feedback HR specialists received after the event left them unsatisfied, raising questions on how to address the issues they uncovered. Some employees found the format of the entire event less productive than expected, like a mix of empty talks and in-depth reviews. Some mentioned the newcomer's case with a note 'unfriendly'. And more improvements to think about. The HR plan was to gather a group of community enthusiasts to decide the future of the events. Jenny was among the participants.

None could absolutely say what happened there and what was there in the plan afterwards. Jenny was informed about the feedback from the newcomers' game. With HRs involved, I am sure it was presented in a very diplomatic way, without any pressure, to ensure everyone stayed engaged and loyal to the company. As the action item, Jenny was asked to give a technical speech at the next community events and motivate other women to apply as speakers for the upcoming gatherings.

Who knew how it would affect company culture. Just a month later, the company announced headcount plans driven by new customer projects. For HR and the entire management, this signaled the need for a change. They started an active hiring process world-wide and focused more on people management. Soon after, the company adopted new policies to promote staff development and career planning.

These company changes influenced community meetings too. With team members spread across the globe, a chance to hold events onsite in a single location was impossible. Instead, the online format and technology-specific groups thrived. Among them, the company's women's club stood out as one of the most visited. Also due to Jenny's involvement.

Before it happened, Jenny's career also took another direction. With a new company focus, she wanted to switch to another department in the same company and worked on new products' development. A new assignment required her to take several intensive training programs and fill in knowledge gaps in a short time. In a year's time, she got a recognition from the company leaders on a fantastic career milestone she accomplished as one of the pioneering women who stayed at the foundation of the company.

In parallel, she started volunteering for city initiatives and speaking about women in tech companies. She enrolled herself in various free programs to promote tech careers and mentor those with any concern on starting a career in IT. As an agent of change, she found joy to inspire women by sharing her knowledge and skills.

United by the idea of establishing an in-house women's tech club, Jenny and several other women came together to make it known and heard within the company. And they did it.

What I know from social media, Jenny being a successful female in the IT world, continues doing speeches, enjoying the stage and a microphone, and intensively discussing the technical world complexity and opportunities for women.

You may probably have people in your surrounding who stay involved with their schools, colleges and universities after graduation. And I am not referring to big parties where everyone meets after ten or twenty years of graduation. I am about the case, when being hired employees or entrepreneurs they continue to actively reconnect with their teachers and professors and create a network that may bring them other benefits. This volunteering involvement happens because of different reasons. Many people want to stay connected to their alma mater and give back to them for the career changes that happened in their lives. And here is Alex's story.

I can not think of anyone who could have demonstrated this subject better than Alex, a technical manager in IT, who I was lucky to know. Before I begin, it makes sense to explain the company's attitude toward educational projects. Among other priorities, education and self-growth held a special place in their company mission. Literally, it was felt on every corner of the company. As they kept a printed mission seen in all public places: office cantines and big meeting rooms. Annually the company invested money and people hours to support local and state universities, colleges and schools with infrastructure, furniture and knowledge base. For that, they hired a complete team of specialists to take care of all kinds of training needs, both internal and external.

On all levels, top managers took great pride in being graduates of various math, computer, humanitarian and physic schools and universities. What to say, if they were sending warm greetings to their professors and university heads on social media. Many enrolled their children, supporting a sense of belonging to their educational families. The deep connection to their school and academic roots turned into a strong learning culture that advocated employees to grow and invest in future generations.

Knowing that, local and foreign universities were looking for cooperation and investments. One such joint project was to provide company employees with the opportunities to obtain PhD using resources of a particular university. The initiative had never been attractive to anyone before as it had some specific requirements. To obtain a PhD, one usually has to invest hundreds of hours in discoveries, communication, material preparation, teaching and much more.

For Alex, this project was bigger than a PhD. As a university graduate, he knew how things are in his alma-mater. As the tech industry evolves at the speed of thought, the university knowledge base often struggles to keep pace. The gap between academic knowledge and industry standards grew as a snowball. Upon graduation, Alex, as a permanent mentor, found himself dealing with graduates who were far from the industry requirements. Long time ago he was one of these graduates. And it took him extra effort to catch up the knowledge gaps and reach the heights of the tech world.

Along with research, meeting professors and working on his thesis, he became a part-time teacher for a small salary in his additional job. Usually, his classes took place in the evenings and at weekends. To stay flexible with his main job, he agreed to this initiative as it was live communication with students who required the knowledge from a top specialist like him. The university system could offer nothing similar to what Alex could explain. Alex's knowledge was several miles behind the materials students could get from any other full-time allocated teacher.

After several years working at the university part-time, Alex successfully obtained a PhD and decided to continue his teaching career. Along with the main job that demanded his full attention. To make it work smoothly, Alex developed a series of elearning for his students to access it despite his limited availability. He was driven by an impact he could provide through different educational initiatives flavored with social responsibility messages, similar to Alex's bosses who continued working with educational institutions from various levels to ensure the best possible outcome for students, professors, systems, new generations, and their business.

When I was a part of projects with a focus on social responsibility, I always assessed potential candidates through the lens of their volunteering or social activity in general. My candidates for such projects were among the top people in their companies, who had grown enough and found a mission to volunteer to other people's needs. There were people who truly cared and always brought a sense of purpose to anything they did. I saw people who wanted to find a stage to convey their message.

To my observation, everyone who mentored others, shared their ideas with the younger generation, volunteered to help others in finding their career paths, and so on, was thankful for being involved in such initiatives. It felt like their heads and hearts were full of information, and they just needed to express it somewhere, otherwise, they would explode. They needed a free space again to learn new things and give it back to society.

If you feel the same and have at least one great message for others, express it. In a written or oral form. For a small audience, or for a big public. Good thoughts should be seen and heard. And maybe, they will bring a change to someone's life, as they did already to yours.

CHAPTER 3

THE GREAT ESCAPE

In 2020, in one sitting, I watched the Westworld series produced by the HBO company. The movie describes a fantasy world where humans could join a robot theme park designed by scientists and get new experiences, including those which are otherwise under law restriction.

Each robot in the park has the look and behavior of a typical human being. Despite their difference in height, sex, skin and hair color, there was a basic similarity. They have their roles and own programming settings to let the game play and develop in various directions. Along with the outstanding story of artificial intelligence, actors cast, graphics and general idea, I found one robot character extremely interesting.

At first, this character looked nothing remarkable. She acted pretty normal and according to her non-central role: being unaware of her robot nature and murdered by a human in one of the park facilities. But then, with each new death and rebirth in the laboratory, where she took a complete reset to a default setting, she started having visions. Scenes of her last days at the park and lab with workers talking to each other. That experience intrigued her mind and made her focused more on a learning process she was undertaking each new day in the park.

In a while, this robot character was taken for yet another necessary maintenance, where she finally identified her real scenario. As lab workers told her, the creator of the park programmed her to experience death multiple times to be once awakened in a lab with an understanding of her robot identity and destiny. This destiny, if it is all normal to say in regards to a robot, is to escape from the park to begin her new life in the real environment, a city with humans and robots around.

The episode in the laboratory left me with some questions. Similar to the robot learning every day to stop the game she didn't enjoy anymore, I wondered:

- What actions do I usually take when I start to feel disengaged from my job?
- Is learning my addiction making me kind of a robot alike? Or learning is my identity setting that I need to survive?
- Do I switch my mind from one interesting learning into another because I have the continuer learner's role to play?
- Is there any new identity of me I should still discover through learning?

These are only several of the questions that were popping up in my head until I systematized them into some logic. To my understanding, we are all programmed at birth to learn the entire life. As it opens numerous new doors and introduces us to new possibilities. To make it happen, we have to close old doors to create a space for growth. Even if it means escaping. By naming this chapter *The great escape* I am giving an honor to the human brain for its marvelous ability to protect and lead us towards new challenges. If we assume that humans only use up to ten or so percent of our brain's capability, then I truly understand why we try so hard to exchange boredom for something fun and engaging.

Here you will find examples of why humans want to escape monotonous processes and jobs and how our brains search for new interests and ideas to stimulate our brain activity, curiosity and creativity. To escape boredom, we jump into problem-solving processes and seek innovative solutions, alone or in a group.

Monotony, like many other things in the world, has two sides. Doing repetitive tasks can bring us a feeling of comfort, relaxation and self-efficiency, as we spend less energy on a well-known process and can see things done faster. On the other hand, monotony sits next to boredom and demotivation. Sooner or later, we become disconnected from the process and our brain calls for help and a change of activity.

When I joined the IT industry in 2006, I heard from everywhere that IT is all about challenges. Here you would never hear about problems, as all problems are challenges to be solved. I still wonder if this wording is a part of some manipulation or it is a real industry concept. But I would agree, in IT everything is changing like lightning. Challenges or problems occur every day. Everyone has to be trained to predict and then deal with them in the fastest and smartest way. Being agile is a key skill for success. And this is no industry rumor. It is a complete truth.

Sometimes I felt like there was nothing between a monotony and a challenge. Like, there was no balance and feeling of comfort, where one could relax and get a relief to do a regular job. Later I found the dependency on the corporate culture. If a challenging culture is in the blood of top managers, it will spread across departments. And then, there is everyone's single wish, to escape challenges and finely dive into some routine. At least, for a while.

Another thing I heard from my start was that learning in IT is extremely important. As a former team member of multiple learning and development teams, I could not agree more. Approximately, every six months, I noticed a new framework, approach or technology emerging. Now, with artificial intelligence as a big trend, this cycle is even shorter. Across all company levels, including human resources and learning and development there was always something new to explore if your goal is to stay on the top.

The words *sameness* and *monotony* are often associated with apathy, dullness, and no variety. We use these words to express our emotions caused by some activities, be it work or communication:

-   It's a monotonous process to do the same task every day.
-   The same type of job makes me feel bored.

What could stand behind these words:

-   When working on routine or same-type projects no longer feels fulfilling.

-   When new challenges bring no joy.

-   No interest or adrenaline left in what someone was doing and where it was happening.

In such cases, the company often responds by offering unplanned vacations, opportunities to attend world-class conferences and workshops if any budget, expanding responsibilities, or retraining employees to try different roles within their competencies.

Compared to vacations or expanding responsibilities, retraining is not as commonly used as a solution. However, it plays a crucial role. As it not only renews employees' interest, but also opens new paths for their gradual development within the company, and in such a way can generate more revenue.

The retraining process, I have observed, unfolded to two scenarios:

1. Officially requested and organized with the help of HRs and learning and development teams. It signals an open culture that encourages honest feedback, making it clear when things are not okay on the employee side.

2. Unofficial. When an employee decides to take this road alone without informing their managers. This happens for different reasons. Among those are fear of rejection, self-doubt about the chosen path, poor learning culture, and hesitation to express what truly drives them more than a recent assignment or a promoted position.

Both scenarios could lead to success or not – for an employee and a company. When leadership actively supports the transformation by providing resources and guidance, many retraining processes yield bigger outcomes for both the employee and the company.

I have witnessed amazing transformations, driven by a company's strong support and commitment to a learning culture. From recruiter to delivery manager, from testing engineer to developer, from HR to department manager, all these changes did not happen at once. Each path was definitely unique, full of challenges and rewards.
I also know several cases when doors to a new role did not open. And extra time invested in retraining seemed nothing valuable. All this brought exhaustion and disappointment on all sides. Sometimes, though, the inspiration could come from where they would not expect it. Like, trying out entirely different roles within a company. For others, completing the retraining program prepared them to step outside the company.

Hard to say, if these transformations I mentioned above started with a feeling of boredom only. My guess is that better career and long-term opportunities, combined with salary compensations and the desire to break up monotonous tasks with more engaging projects, were among key factors driving the decision.

Sameness can result in lacking a change in regards to other people, when someone reacts strangely or ignores what we do or ask. To my observation, this usually happens with over-skilled workers, different from people who never came to fit the corporate culture. Or those who have already outgrown themselves in a particular company and try to bring improvements at any level but get permanent rejection or neglect. This is not the case of loyal and creative people whose ideas are relevant, but their quantity overloads managers. Then these managers seek to evade or communicate *No* in the best possible way. I am talking about the cases where people try to escape from a constant feeling of being useless, unheard, unrecognized, and so on. This feeling, when constant, can present as boredom. And sooner or later, they escape it by becoming silent. By diving into some new learning. Or finding their new place to be valuable again outside the company.

Sometimes we try to escape from somewhere or something and use learning as a solution to stay busy; hide from unwanted truths and our insecurities; solve issues that are out of our responsibility. We bring our ideas into places that are not ready for that. As our work standards and values differ.

Listen to the story of Evan who has been with his company for four years. As a single person in his position, he took responsibility for a scope of tasks related to managing and maintaining networks, infrastructure, and providing first-level support for employees. Like many technology consultants, self-learning became a regular part of his weekly routine. He was hungry for technological novelties, and being alone in his role, he was forced to search for technical solutions himself. In several consecutive years, Evan's workload grew to the sky. He got calls and emails non-stop. His company management was rarely interested in his growth. No one thought to support him with opportunities for obtaining new skills and replacement for vacation time. That was not a priority, as Evan was always busy and never complained too much. He was a single hero on a battlefield with numerous projects on his plate.

This job kept him focused and motivated. Each day was completely new compared to the previous one. Boredom was not a word from Evan's vocabulary. The adrenaline he got, unfortunately, had a back side. After another tough week full of stress, Evan felt sick. Spending three days in bed with a terrible headache and muscle pain, he faced an unpleasant truth: the unstoppable routine coming to him was caused by blurred company standards, poor processes and lack of clarity on responsibilities. He started reflecting on dozens of cases where he brought improvements and crystal clear ideas on how to manage various situations. For small things, it worked. But most of the time, with big and important solutions, he got back pointless conversation and lack of understanding from the management. He was disappointed in the company and himself. And for the first time he did not want to go to the office at all.

Having gathered strength, he found the solution, as he thought. His finding led him to the idea of upgrading his soft skills. He wanted to feel more confident talking to his managers and finally solve the situation as it was getting worse with each month.

By setting aside time and paying from his own pocket, he enrolled himself into several online courses to enhance his management skills. All that gave him hope for change he could bring to the company with his new and strong voice. After completing a set of courses, it did not work as he expected. The more he spoke to his bosses, convincing them to hire several new people to his team, apply new technologies, save budgets where applicable and so on, the worse their communication became. It seemed like Evan was talking to a brick wall ignoring every word he expressed. The company simply wanted him to ensure that all employees' requests were addressed and that no infrastructure issues occurred. But that was far from reality and his potential. Evan was already deeply burnt out, but did not want to admit it.

Upset and exhausted after several attempts to prove his point to the management, he was terribly offended. All the solutions he could offer failed to address the core of the problem. In a while, taking some time to reflect on the things going on, he quit.

After a short sabbatical, he joined another company, dealing with complex issues, learning from his peers and managers, and feeling less stressed than before. Boredom, in a good sense, has become something appreciated, which gives time to reflect and do monotonous work. He alternates between boredom and complicated tasks, where he proves his proficiency and super energy.

You probably know people who do the same job from day to day for many years, and are fine with it. I personally see nothing bad in routine. I know that changes and a variety of tasks can ruin people's feeling of predictability and calmness. They value security and stability in their work processes and communication. What sounds boring for one, may look like a craziness for another. If you are a people manager, you should recognise the difference in values.

For some time, I had a question similar to the previously explored legacy issue: how does escaping sameness relate to age? I observe that the younger we are, the more we need novelties and opportunities to try new things. On the other hand, the older we get, the more we want stability and security in our jobs and learning. But this correlation is not linear. Our personalities, energy levels and bigger values behind may influence us too.

If you work in, or are somehow connected to social media, marketing or application development, you should be familiar with gamification. In learning and development, gamification started long ago. You probably remember these times, when training mostly happened in a room with trainees and trainers. And where a flipchart with colored pens and stickers served as a whiteboard to visualize ideas, questions, learners' progress, and so on. Trainers offered games and small gifts to enhance learners' engagement and drive them to a desired outcome.

Later, gamification took an online format of personalized learning journeys with digital badges, points, leaderboards, multiple level quizzes, and so on. What used to happen onsite found its new meaning and format online to keep remote users engaged.

Gamification became a process of applying different techniques to make learning effective in the digital environment. The task *engagement* turned into a real challenge for learning teams. Sometimes mixed with fun, the purpose of making content engaging produces overcomplicated training scenarios with no impact on learners' success. Studies confirm: the process of remembering things goes better when our interest level is high. To achieve this in learning, modern learning software may enroll learners in a game, give them an association to remember, change content formats, play a video, ask for feedback, personalize content, and much more. If none of this happens, users may get bored fast, and their interest and motivation to finish learning comes to zero. Our memory decides to stop working, and our brain switches to something different, more entertaining to do now, as the brain sees it.

My strong opinion here is, not every piece of content should be entertaining and look like a silly movie. The key is in keeping balance and aligning gamification with course objectives and audience needs. And in some cases, having live training with a flip chart can serve better.

My first gamified course looked pretty simple. I used one of the content authoring tools to create the learning material as an animated movie. I learnt how characters interacted with each other, how design blocks and elements worked together, how audio completed the video, and a lot more. That was fun, I must admit. I spent hours in a hotel room playing and learning from it. Now I assume that the time it took me to learn the tool would have been different if the format of learning had required me to read manuals and answer multiple quizzes. In this case, the gamification led me the right way to adapt and practice with my projects faster.

Here is another example of gamification.

I have never been a fan of computer games, but I used to know people who are passionate about them and creatively use their functionalities in their work projects. Like Sasha, who I have been friends with for many years. As a programming expert and a big fan of games and continuous development, he was the one to customize learning management systems, mentor newbies, drive local community and continue coding in different languages in parallel.

It had happened to him before, when he became tired with his regular work assignments. But this time was special. Sasha lost all enthusiasm and nothing seemed to bring joy anymore. Luckily for him, his boredom turned into something extremely productive.
He took some time to shuffle his interests, company needs, existing skills and the skills he wanted to acquire. At the end, his brain yielded him an unexpected fit of creativity. While talking to one of his colleagues, they both remembered an online gamified framework Coding Dojo. That conversation became an inspiration that lasted an entire decade.

Driven by three passions, programming, gaming and networking, Sasha and his colleague adjusted the framework and made the process of learning exciting and captivating for programmers in a specific for the company field. They created a learning environment where game participants are eager to try different strategies and simulations, collaborate with their teammates and enjoy the process of playing the famous Tetris and later the Snake game first invented in 1976.

Highly supported by management, these two were developing and organizing games for their colleagues to stimulate intellectual activity for several years in a row.

When I heard of his new passion, I remembered all the stories of programmers who ensured me: all the brain wants after a long coding day is to have relaxation and fun. No more routine tasks. To get this fun, IT brains play computer and board games, multiply complex numbers in their head, do sports, and just relax the way they like. Unlike many mobile or computer games that might be considered by skeptics a waste of time, this framework brought meaningful benefits.

As a true follower of computer games, Sasha decided to make the development process exciting for himself too. Well, who will care of an author if not himself? And he cared. To say more, I have been to his home to see the workplace. To be fully present and laser-focused on the game objectives and scenarios, he converted his working room sofa into a desk. In order to keep himself comfortable, he used a special construction to keep his laptop in a specific position and worked lying on his back. When I asked about this invention, he justified it as a convenience for his back, which gives him pain from time to time.

After several years of local company gatherings over this game, Sasha and his colleague started organizing championships among programmers using the framework. These championships spread beyond company doors and became available for any community willing to host these events in their venues or online.

This story could be one of many about investing money into the project with a big potential in it. However, it did not happen. Instead, it ended after twelve years, teaching me how to make fun of games while two tech minds worked together to break free from their work routine.

Where is Sasha now? In 2025, he explores new territory of artificial intelligence he has never worked too closely with before. There is a spark of curiosity the way he approaches it – a playful side that has not faded over time. It is still there, guiding him to try new things out, see what works, and uncover what is possible. It is never just about learning. For him, it is about a sense of wonder and seeing where it leads to.

Hard to imagine the time where gamification of learning turns into something old-fashioned. Nowadays, new technologies bring to us more and more various learning formats and tools, where gamification, together with design and personalized scenarios, proves its effectiveness. My guess, we will continue entering the fun zone to get the best out of learning. Just the fun will vary and become more technology-based.

However, it is important to consider the nature of people, who are not triggered by games. They will not value your digital badges, avatars and modern web design. Instead, they will probably prefer to participate in quizzes, low interaction games and some other activities.

Several times I have been invited to co-organise hackathons. Originally from the technology community, hackathons became a special type of event that unites people for a twenty-four or forty-eight-hour search for solutions.

Some of us pretend to be busy in public. With work and life stuff we leave us almost no time to explore, experiment and try new things. So hackathons, with their specific timing and format, allow participants to feel like they were in a real marathon. Gathered in groups, people with different skills and backgrounds can generate creative solutions, design prototypes, and present their ideas to a jury. And like in any contest, the jury decides on winners and prizes to support participants' efforts and mastery.

All hackathons that I witnessed in my career were for and from the IT world. They aimed to search for tech solutions and modern ideas in various fields, like e-commerce, automotive, healthcare, and many more. The biggest excitement of hackathons for me was the variety of ideas participants could generate together in such a short time. With every hackathon, I was telling myself: Wow, and how big are the dimensions of *possible*? How big are the capacities of the human brain?

I have been to student and corporate hackathons in different years. In both cases, I have observed a synergy between people gathered for a single purpose.

How they differ from one another is why most students and staff teams come to participate. Speaking of students, they were attracted to the novelty of the event. They got inspired by the idea of a new community, challenges, work chances, venue and even a branded merchandise collection they would get after. The hackathon, whose very name was unknown to many students, was an opportunity to get all this at once and stand out from friends. I met students who were driven by the idea of making this world better with their inventions.

What I never saw in students was a need to escape monotony. This need was evident at corporate hackathons, which were organized for proficient technology consultants, in their mid-thirties and forties, with numerous projects, skills, jobs and life challenges in their portfolios. Having routine types of jobs or the opposite, stressy and messy roles, they were looking for a break from standard work life. For some of them, hackathons were necessary to stay updated on the industry and technological enhancements, to focus on a single task, to meet new people and learn from their experiences. For those who spent many years on big enterprise projects with no end in sight, the hackathon gave a desired feeling of things done in twenty four or forty eight hours. For some of them, the hackathon was like fresh air and a reminder of a light and passion they could bring into their jobs.

Hackathons are usually group events, and I would like to share a story of one of them.

There were these guys, a group of university students, who first heard of a hackathon from one of their professors. As it usually happens, in every group someone takes a leader's role. In this case, it was a young guy, let us call him Andrew, who was truly passionate about software and technology since his childhood.

The intent to join the hackathon immediately stuck in his mind. He spent one of his evenings learning more about the format and started reflecting on the ideas they could present as a team. Later on, he discovered the hackathon organizers offered a money prize along with mentorship support to guide the winner's team work on a project and maximize their success. All that heated up his motivation to win.

Andrew got together with his university friends and they split responsibilities according to their strengths. One guy became a mobile developer, another one covered the design part, and yet another felt confident with marketing and sales. Everyone agreed to have Andrew as chief. The group brainstormed in one of their student dorm rooms, where Andrew brought paper and pens to visualize all the ideas, trying to repeat some scenes he'd seen in movies. They spent several evenings together, feeling comfortable with each other and inspired.

The project they brought to the hackathon surprised the jury and left all other groups behind. None of them at that moment expected to see among the students' finalists socially responsible ideas of business. For Andrew, however, the project went beyond marketing and student level events. With their participation, Andrew targeted more than the jury committee. He wanted to run a business and the hackathon triggered his leadership skills, entrepreneurship spirit and learning mindset trained well in his university projects. The young people agreed on investing money from the hackathon in developing a mobile application.

The team's life split into two: before and after the hackathon. Everything went out from being content. It was a real business. As promised to them on the hackathon, they requested help from the sponsoring company and took their consultancy hours. The time spent with the company experts was highly beneficial, as it revealed many gaps in their business plan. This collaboration offered Andrew and his team a fresh perspective and enabled them with a strategic focus going forward.

As for the hackathon organizing company, this initiative was not new. They already had experience of participating and organizing similar events in cooperation with tech companies and big educational institutions. On one hand, it was a long-term strategy to collaborate with universities and to help them spread creativity and invention mindset among young talents. On the other hand, the company planned to set up its own startup department to support beginner and proficient entrepreneurs and their promising projects in the company's portfolio.

Back to the hackathon winners. After fixing the gaps in the business plan and technology backside, they continued their journey at a bigger startup contest. Andrew and his friend, skilled in marketing, pitched their project to a new jury aiming to win a money prize and be recognised in the media. They swept yet another hackathon, proving again how a youth could be lucky. Next was an active product development phase and other contests, pitches, conferences, where they absorb knowledge from business and technology gurus.

It took up to two years of active development and marketing to be finally recognised on the state level and get investments from one of the local business accelerators.
What started once as a five minute chit chat with a professor, moved into a dormitory room with a flipchart, grew up to a real company with real people and revenue. It is a story when a combination of a good idea, creative team, perfect time could bring them all to new horizons that no one had even dared to imagine. This story Andrew shared with students across the country, who wanted to learn about his path from student to entrepreneur.

It sounds like a happy ending and not. Some years ago I discovered from social media that the startup story ended with the company's closure. The message Andrew shared with his followers said nothing about the reasons behind this decision, which I assume were more than tough. During a year, he focused on charging his own batteries, self-reflection and planning the future. He finished his message emphasizing the importance of taking time for personal well-being. Matured and full of optimism, he was already into something remarkable in the tech world, asking everyone to stay tuned for his updates.

From the time I first tried hackathon and until now, I have seen continuous interest in this kind of event as a format, and I understand why. It allows people with technology and entrepreneurship values to get together and solve real-life cases. Even a long time with no sleep, with caffeine overdose, sometimes uncomfortable chairs, desks, lack of food and so on, will non stop the youth or adults willing to explore their brain resource limits, find like-minded people or maybe a million-dollar business idea.

Whatever role you take, an organiser or a participant, it is a great opportunity to re-energise and refocus. If you work for a business, you can implement this format and hold a hackathon in a shorter time, for a particular group of employees, like leaders only, with a concrete business focus, or a moderator leading the group towards their goal. Being in a participant's shoes is the best way to experience the format from the inside out and inject a boost of motivation into your daily business.

Long time ago I considered success as a final destination. If I am done with a project, it leads me to my so-called success, which is determined by a number of criteria. I visualized success as me standing on the top of a mountain. Later, I started considering success as a process, similar to catching a wave and smoothly riding my surf no matter what was going on around. This journey on a wave made me feel extremely happy. This happiness is what I thought a pure success should feel like.

My next insight on success was in having it as a trained habit. I explained success as a mix of different elements and soft skills, like discipline, continued learning, resilience, positive thinking, a special type of mindset, and much more. All this allowed me to come to the idea that success for me is no less than a combination of them all: a final outcome, along with a continuous process, and a strongly developed habit. Together they move me towards another me, different from who I have been before.

My understanding of success is closely connected to change at all levels, should it be my skills, surroundings or my personality. If you read this and thought of my extreme confidence, I will disappoint you. On my way to a new achievement and a change, I have been feeling anxious half of the time.

You know this feeling. When the brain pictures you with good and bad images of what could happen next. Luckily, in many cases good images win against bad ones. And bad ones help us to identify risks and worse case scenarios. Then we can act according to our initial plan and fear less. In some cases, we feel our incompetence and are afraid of being exposed. Many things explained as imposter syndrome are well known to many of us. When we investigate the subject, we find many layers underneath, including the one that relates to fear of success or result.

In my work and surroundings I often notice people who are hungry for learning. They look passionate and nothing seems to stop them from achieving their goals. I felt proud meeting this kind of people, who were inspiring role models to me. But what I did not know is that in some cases there were masks hiding an unpleasant truth. This truth is in being afraid to achieve something meaningful or big in their lives. All this learning happens to fill the gap and prove to others, and specifically themselves, how hard they try, how much they invest in learning, and how patiently they wait for the time when this desired success will finally come.

You probably know someone who is trying to switch into another field or job and takes numerous courses and master classes for years. But no change happens because of lack of knowledge, confidence, good endorsements, favorable market conditions, and many other reasons announced.
You may know a person who has been learning a language for years and still cannot speak, explaining it by being bad at languages, changing teachers, lack of methodology, and their bad memory.

You could ask then, what kind of inevitable change may happen to people? I assume that for those afraid of change or success, there might be several scenarios, like:

1. A change will happen in a while. It is a matter of time and the person's level of dissatisfaction with the current situation. The change can be triggered by an inner process or come with the help of a trainer, consultant, coach, friend, whoever else.

2. A change will be reevaluated and take another format. For instance, if they are considering becoming a specialist in a particular field with the help of some courses, they intentionally turn their path into another field, where all their obtained skills will be finally acceptable or monetised.

3. All investments in learning are made to get an answer, like: *I have had enough of spending money and energy on this. I quit.* In this scenario a change takes place as an insight to stop the hamster wheel.

In my jobs and coaching practice, I met people who took one or several roads to make a change. In the first and second scenarios, their willingness to succed won over their level of anxiety or perfectionism. A level of dissatisfaction with the current situation got so high that allowed them to make a step towards their true desires and success. The third scenario is important too, as it finally turns into a concrete solution to stop investing into something that does not work. There is no choice between best and worst. They all matter and are applicable in different life and career situations.

It so happened that I have been involved in numerous projects aiming at attracting junior level talents through the career opportunities available in the company. Usually such projects transform into events to gather numerous people interested in joining the tech industry and work with modern technologies. There were recent students and graduates of technical and mathematical universities and colleges. And those who the industry call *switchers*.

These are the individuals with no special tech education seeking to start their new careers by switching from industries like retail, automotive, and others. In my memory, these events stand out for the number of switchers who attended not so much for the presentations, but for the support and reassurance that they could successfully move forward. They were looking for conversations to prove that success was possible despite any circumstances including their age. As there were people of different age groups including forties and fifties whose anxieties often weighed heavily. And sometimes even overshadowed their ambitions.

Here is a story of Diana. A mom, in her mid-forties, who was
in search of herself.
Her university years were not much different from her friends.
They all tried to work evenings or weekends in small
businesses to get cash money and spent it on themselves or
leisure time. For Diana, her part-time job as an office
administrator in the IT company from her university time
became a steady job for many years. Following graduation,
she felt extremely comfortable working in a well-known
environment like her company. Everything and everyone
looked like a family.

After marrying and becoming a mom, nothing much changed
for her. The company allowed Diana to work remotely when
necessary, so that she could take care of her family and kids
and give them a homemade cookie treat. She got a little
money from the company to invest in herself and kids. That
was fine for her as she stayed in the comfortable place with
not much stress. In a while, she even tried herself as an
administrative project manager. The place was open to offer
her new possibilities to grow and feel recognition.

Things changed as the kids grew up. At their five and seven
they had their first work orientation classes. Bringing
numerous questions home about different jobs, the kids

triggered Diana's deeply hidden thoughts: How long is she planning to stay in this studio? Is it her career limit in this life? What role model does she make for her children? These questions haunted her.

After a while, she became curious about different design jobs as it could satisfy her passion for drawing and crafting. It promised her a better salary and career opportunities especially in the tech area.

Determined to succeed, Diana joined numerous online classes to become a designer. She was attracted to all kinds of courses, from interaction design to 3D modeling and more. She was scared to confess about the new study at her company. So, she decided to take the learning at her own path.

Despite struggles with learning new technologies and completing massive homework assignments, she approached each course with a true dedication and a big hope. After each course, her motivation grew, but did not last long. A month or two after, she would start feeling anxiety, believing she was not capable of moving forward.

It looked like she stepped into her shoe closet where each pair promised her something new and great but ended in disappointment. To test her hypothesis of whether it suited her, she imagined different careers throughout her life. The first pair of shoes makes her role too small for her ambitions; the second one could bring much stress to her family; the third one was out of her dreams at all. Each try she did showed her yet another challenge of finding the right path for her career and identity.

Every time she was ready to make a step towards her goal, something happened in her company or in the family that required her to refocus and manage these obstacles rather than applying for a new job. She could not even prepare her resume as she felt incompetent and miserable having a single work experience mentioned. In her thoughts, she compared herself to potential candidates and found numerous gaps in her knowledge telling her she should better continue learning rather than just start a career.

The impostor syndrome paired with continuous learning held her back for several years. It lasted until once she watched a culinary TV show where a middle-aged lady, a former manager in tech, looking similar to Diana, passionately described her path to pastries. Working at home because of her two kids, a lady from the show was able to get income through baking. That show had an impressive effect on Diana. As she devoted her evenings and weekends to the family cooking and baking time. She finally connected the dots and decided to look in this direction rather than design in IT itself.

In a year of practicing at home, she had developed a unique cooking style that combined techniques from her learning time and the best of her family recipes. Her company work ended when the owner decided to close his office in this city. The time to enter the dark finally came.
That fact shifted Diana's search for fulfillment onto a new road. With two kids at home and the level of comfort she cherished, she had no passion to become a hired employee. Instead, she began to consider the opportunity of running a

small business as an owner. Similar to the lady from the TV show.

Her pastries became a family speciality, so she decided to share her work at school events in her neighborhood. Two school-age kids offered her plenty of opportunities to gather feedback. Teachers, parents and other kids who tried her pastries enjoyed the taste and the custom packaging design. It looked no different from those in the supermarket but with much better taste.

That feedback was a signal to continue and think of opening a local pastry shop to fulfill Diana's dream. Her family became her full support to help with legal and administration tasks, while she was totally into baking and pastries. Her design skills and years spent on learning gave her a strong foundation to be successful. Her first official shop started as a social media page. Later it grew into an online shop and finally a pastry storefront opened in her own name.

Hard to say whether it is fortunate or not, but not all stories end like this one. Many end with less output. It can take many years of struggling until something crucial happens to beat the anxiety. Anxiety, like many other emotions of ours, has its benefits. In other words, we want to feel anxious not to start or progress with our goals and projects. The day we find the answer to what our anxiety really means can become a day of insight, when the desired project may get off the ground.

CHAPTER 4

COLLECTIVE INTELLIGENCE

I can not name a business, be it a big corporation or a family entrepreneurship, where collective intelligence brings no value to owners. Any successful business coming to my mind, from a product manufacturer to a call center, has a need to cultivate a culture of thinking outside the box, documenting and sharing best practices, and growing innovation mindset. Would it be implemented in a particular team, department, or the entire company.

We all know IQ (intelligence quotient) tests for measuring individuals' intelligence. They are widely used to assess our abilities to think, memorize and recognize. There are no standards to measure a company's collective intelligence. Just imagine, to get the accurate data you would need to involve the entire company and assess their engagement, collaboration, problem-solving approaches and many other criterias for quite a while. Could be an interesting project with huge investments.

When I talk about collective intelligence in tech, I usually think of three approaches:

1. A people-driven approach.
When we gather people for a meeting, like a brainstorm session, online or onsite to accumulate their ideas, thoughts, feedback, etc. At the end of the session, we usually expect a list of items, solutions to work further.

2. A technology-based approach.

When a company implements various digital tools, like Productboard, Confluence, Notion, or Wiki for sharing ideas, feedback, notes, comments, and insights. These tools engage employees, partners and customers to continuously collect their ideas. With numerous people involved, these tools help everyone save time on numerous meetings. With these tools in place, all stakeholders can easily be informed and make decisions with more clarity and purpose.

3. Mixed approach.

The one that combines people-driven and technology-based approaches and takes the best of both. From a learning culture perspective, when these two work together in the company, this could bring significant results in business.

Across various meetings and projects in tech aimed at supporting collective intelligence concept, I have gathered several observations to share with you:

- When I have been a part of a cross-team gathering with a broad audience, we were able to get to the root of the problem in a short time and create a list of outstanding solutions.

There are many book cases where people from different teams gathered together become a powerful source of creativity. Simply by coming from different company departments, which might look unrelated at first. Yet, within a single organization, each team contributes to the same big goals. And a synergy through diverse perspectives makes these gatherings so resourceful.

- A well-known brainstorming technique is still super powerful. Every time, at the end of each session, I was surprised by the outcome, as it showed the full power of collective thinking and challenged creativity.

When we think of a typical brainstorm session, we usually expect a list of ideas as a general result. To my observation, even an abstract outcome, hardly documented on paper and lacking in detail, can lead to significant changes in business.

- Every action item you have after the session requires a follow up effort.

I have been to a situation where all outcomes were left aside. Either on a whiteboard paper, in a google document, or on a task board. Why does the team's motivation drop? The energy was burnt on the session itself. Nothing left to follow through the ideas afterward. The most important part of the session is to ensure the action items' future: what do we want to implement and who will work to make it possible.

- You need to keep skeptical people on board.

Maybe it sounds a bit strange, but the most creative and working solutions were generated together with people, who had a strong critical thinking skill. Some will call them negative for their direct comments. Others will think of them as blocking any idea and team dynamics with numerous questions. There is a truth behind it. Mostly, I have seen a benefit from all kinds of comments and questions, as that led a group into the right direction because of a diverse mindsets.

- Make this planned.

People in big tech companies are always busy. And yet another meeting, especially one focused on brainstorming and idea generation, can often feel like wasted time. Best if these meetings are recurrent. Spontaneous gatherings have their own charm too and a potential to achieve more.

A learning and development team actively promotes collective intelligence in the company, and at some point manages it. Together with leaders at all levels, learning specialists are involved in cultivating a learning mindset and collaboration across the organization. As managers, they can administer platforms for open communication and learning, take care of training assets and support with different requests.

With collective intelligence, the ability to learn from in-house or industry failures, together with customers' voices, is crucial.

One of my favorite project parts was in getting people together for learning purposes. First, for a few employees sharing an office room for one evening hour. Later, within big conferences, contests and online gatherings for a wider audience. Both experiences showed me many times how people across the industry adored speeches in the *lesson learnt* format, when a speaker opens up in front of the audience and presents a business case that failed for different reasons.

Along with a confession in public, speakers usually presented solutions and ideas how they put the fire out, what tools and approaches they used to avoid big losses, and how they would act if the situation repeated.

It felt to me, looking at people's faces, that such kinds of stories were truly emotional for both speakers and attendees. First, the speakers were still reflecting while speaking. The real storm has subsided and is now completely safe to share all the flops and slips. Second, there is no worry about the impact, as it is no more scary to confess. Best time to finally feel *you are a Superman* who made a mistake, but turned our world to the better.

Attendees looked like movie fans at a famous blockbuster premiere. I could not count the number of *Oh man!* and *Hmm* I heard, disguised as smiles and laughter. This laughter was no less than *how good it did not happen to me.*

Let us be honest, none of us likes failing. Anyone who tells us that we need to fail to learn is not telling us about the part where we feel guilty, ashamed, confused, unprofessional, and sorrowful. We would rather learn about risks and other people's experiences from such events than step on the same rake and feel the full range of unpleasant emotions.

I was always thankful to speakers who agreed to present such topics to an audience. As I knew, the interest would be higher than in anything theoretical or marketing alike. I was glad to see this format growing up from in-house presentations to big conferences talking of failures only. The more we learn from other people's failures the better we prepare for any uncertainties and challenges. This was probably the idea of the Anticonfence organizers who brought together speakers talking about their failures the entire day. Kudos to organizers who found a proper name for it.

This format looked different from the many typical events with marketing and sales presentations. The biggest gift to me as an organizer was to welcome tech leaders and managers presenting their failures. It was possible to make all this public only with learning cultures open to failures. The purpose of such stories is to prevent similar cases in the future, facilitate productive discussion, and build collective intelligence. And surely not to publicly insult engineers, clients and other stakeholders for the decisions they made one day.

Every time I listened to top managers' speeches, I noticed interesting things. I can not name them steady patterns, but they happened every time in my experience. The most obvious observation, both online and onsite presentations from company tops gathered maximum people. While typically, around thirty percent of people skip events for various reasons, in top managers' cases the enrolment and participation levels were pretty equal.

My next finding, if any video recording was provided, it became one of the top viewed videos in the company archive. Employees regularly asked for it, shared it with each other, and took it as a reference for their skill development, like presentation, design, moderation skills, and so on.

A week or two after a presentation, regardless of the topic, either the entire company or a certain group of employees continued their reflection on the presentation subject. It was so because top managers' speeches always brought an important message to people: What really matters to business? What should you avoid doing? Or opposite, what should you start doing immediately? This key message would become a focus for leaders and managers for the near future. If a top manager confesses to a failure in public, there is something hugely important behind it. So, either read between the lines, or again read between the lines to get a piece of wisdom.

What I also saw in these confessions is yet another message to leaders and managers: *True, our society is obsessed with success. But we are human and sometimes make mistakes to learn from them and become stronger and more adaptable. As a leader, be brave to notice a problem and solve it before it gets out of control.*
I think for many leaders who work under pressure for years, this was important to hear from their bosses in public.

Something that might not happen in one-on-one meetings could happen in public and serve as a long-term motivation.

Collective intelligence is the thing for enterprise and product companies. How is it different for each of the two? In tech enterprise companies it is a tool for accumulating employees' insights and internal groups' knowledge through collaborative decision-making, solving complex issues and driving innovation spirit that is spread across different departments, customer projects and company initiatives.

In tech product companies, collective intelligence is one of the key instruments to gather customer feedback that will later be incorporated in the company's product roadmap. Customers and partners' voices, heard as pains and gains, can directly influence product requirements, development deadlines and budget investments. Along with customer voices, industry and market trends also impact the product roadmap and dictate whether and when company improvements or new developments are to happen.

Customer satisfaction surveys, special events, one-on-one meetings and many other tools serve companies in accumulating collective wisdom. Among these, customer and partner advisory councils stand ahead of others.

But first, I need to explain why this type of business event takes place in this book. The advisory councils I have seen all look like a training event, where a small group of strategically important customers and partners get together for a workshop to learn from different speakers, mainly industry leaders. The participants represented various domains, levels of expertise with the product, business regions, and even their contract values. The idea of having a council lies in the company's need of regular checkups, shared use cases and ideas, voting for product refinements, and collaborating on business challenges. These advisory councils can be organized on the entire company level or serve needs of a particular team, like sales or business development.

Advisory councils serve both parties' needs. For the company-organizer, it is a tool to get important customers together and shape the direction of business. On the other hand, council members can partner with their council peers, other industry leaders, learn from their successes and failures, influence market dynamics, and build a competitive advantage in the fast-changing business.

It was a big question for me, how companies operating on the same market and being often competitors, could come together to peacefully brainstorm their challenges in the same room. As the information from such meetings could potentially be used to gain an advantage over one another.

Later I found that the way the company-organizer creates the atmosphere and agenda matters a lot.

- When the agenda is communicated to all participants in advance, it brings much more outcomes to everyone involved.

It sounds like something obvious. In reality, many events for partners and customers I have observed, looked like yet another marketing event to promote new tech product functionality. With advisory councils, this will not work. An agenda, much like in any training program, should always align with the goals of all involved parties. Workshors and similar training formats work perfect for that audience. To announce marketing updates there should be another channel of communication.

At advisory councils, which I know, all happened behind closed doors, meaning that the outcome of each gathering was never announced to the public as is. Even inside one company, only a particular group of people had access to ideas and use cases presented. I guess that the feeling of a secure environment was truly important for the company and council members.

- If a moderator from the organizing company knows the audience and their specific business challenges.

A moderator or facilitator, preferably not from the top management of the company, can create a safe and collaborative atmosphere, where participants can open up and discuss relevant issues. The more senior the participants, the more strategic questions you can explore. The more participants act as speakers, the more engagement you can get.

- When these events are driven by a company that values a learning extending beyond its employees to partners and customers.

Having a business idea in the ground, these events serve different purposes. Among those I see a need of building a community of experts willing to learn and share from one another to drive success in their fields. A company with a strong learning culture could extract maximum value from these events. If your company operates within a growth mindset, learns from all possible sources including its own failures, and supports readiness for advancement, it might be a sign to look at the advisory councils as one of the collective intelligence generators.

Being a huge fan of individual learning, I do not skip opportunities to learn in groups, as I know the best of both worlds. In an individual approach, I value my flexibility and time spent on reflecting and practicing things that are truly important for me personally. From group learning, I take the dynamics, rhythm, and focus time. And of course, I learn from other people's ideas and their key takeaways. All this extends my understanding of the subject and of this world.

What format does collective intelligence take in your company? Maybe it is a documented knowledge base. Or you manage internal clubs to share knowledge and allow employees to speak about their failures. Think of how it can be implemented within your area of responsibility, as it will bring you significant results in implementing a learning culture.

It is not the most intellectual of the species that survives; it is not the strongest that survives; but the species that survives is the one that is able best to adapt and adjust to the changing environment in which it finds itself.
According to Darwin's Origin of Species.

Our life is full of challenges and uncertainties. None of us can predict with complete confidence what will happen tomorrow. Take weather forecasts – with tons of equipment, they are still not really good at their predictions.
To manage our negative feelings caused by uncertainties, we save extra money, buy insurances, grow our contact networks, do learning, and so on. Learning and its post-effects in particular can become one of the tools to effectively overcome obstacles and get us a feeling of security and comfort. As one of humans' basic needs, security means being certain of what is going on and knowing how to make ourselves feel better, or at least not worse.

You all might know people who work their entire life for a single company. Such stories made me guess that among their values, comfort, loyalty, stability or predictability should be standing somewhere at the top of the priority list. I can truly understand all the benefits of working for a single company for so many years: familiar environment, processes, people, clear opportunities, attractive retirement programs, corporate culture, and other social benefits. Being loyal to one company for so long allows them to maintain financial compensation, bonuses, promotions at all management levels and stay certain that any question will most likely be resolved. As a strategy, working for one employer your entire life can be effective – until hard economic or social times come to create uncertainty.

Twice I have been a witness to world job market crises. And surely I have my own story of what these events taught me. After the fire was out, I had a chance to speak to different people in tech about the lessons they had learned from that time.
Here is what I understood: most of us who were there, remembered this time with sorrow and gratitude, where learning was a key part of these memories.

Most lay-offs begin unexpectedly. And that brought a lot of uncertainties and a high level of stress. Everyone I spoke to had their own way of coping. The most trained ones took a break. Putting the immediate job search on pause, they started looking at the world, industry and even local job trends first. For that, they used different hints from the web and artificial intelligence tools helping them to check world job and skills' trends across industries. I already knew something existed for free but I could not even imagine the number of such tools and platforms. Using that data, people I have spoken to, listed their skills to see where exactly they wanted and could grow. In parallel, they looked at how else they could extend their current profile. In such a way they wanted to get a sense of control and understand the new environment. The environment, which was not easy, if not impossible, to control.

Under stress, our brains could try to calm us down by seeking something entertaining rather than extending our expertise. Some really forced themselves to start retraining. Most of whom I was speaking to were driven by their willpower to finish learning and align its results with evolving market needs. With a new confidence, they began applying for roles that matched their new or extended expertise.

We can consider this a reputation issue. Or a situation when employees return to former employers after time away. But I have heard stories of former employers allowing their laid-off employees to continue learning on their company platforms to gain new skills. They offered free coupons and discounts for their paid programs and certifications to support their next job search. In some cases, former colleagues stepped in as mentors, helping their peers develop new skills. This was all made possible within a well-developed corporate and learning culture that continues to support growth, even after someone leaves the company.

The world crisis is not a single reason to turn on extreme mode. Anything that influences the job market: a sudden storm in a particular company, industry, or a country of residence can become a trigger. When someone decides to switch to another role inside the company brings one a feeling of stress. When it happened to me, I felt like if not today, then I will miss the opportunity to finally unlock the door that really matters to me. Saying that, I was ready to take risks, experiment with different learning and roles, and leave my comfort zone for a while.

For a company, the extreme mode takes the form of contingency plans for various emergencies and potential crises. Different teams, finance, delivery, human management, and others work together to analyze different scenarios and identify risks and resources to handle this.
Strategic planning is important not only during crises, but also for navigating the changing environment, ensuring the company stays profitable and ahead of trends and new technologies. Let me share some ideas about what companies and individuals do to prevent risk scenarios.

Behind any innovation are people who created it to change the lives of others. We all remember from human history how a new invention occasionally appeared after a genius idea or a failed experiment which turned into success. We have heard stories of scientists who devoted their lives to projects making it their daily routine.

In big tech companies, there are special teams, like research and development laboratories, resource teams, and similar company structures to support this and other functions. Companies can hire people for full-time roles or allocate team members temporarily to experiment with a new technology, create prototypes, develop custom tools and frameworks, and many more.

Fear of being left behind and stagnating can be one of the reasons for tech companies to organize such teams on their bases. Nowadays, we hear more often than ever, and from every channel, that only those who innovate stay competitive and survive on the market. Here is a story of one research and development laboratory that functions under one of the IT companies.

It all started at the times when data science and data analytics were just buzzwords for most people – but not for the top management of a tech company. At their level, these words were already poised to be spoken. Organizing a dedicated new department was a bit of an extreme and risky idea. Too high costs to end up with nothing at the end of the project. But experimenting to see the outcomes in a short term was more than doable, with little investment. For that, the management decided to hire mathematically strong students from local universities to work part-time on an internal project. There were no doubts about who would lead the group as there was Brian, their top expert who embodied a complete understanding of math, proficiency with IT technologies and passion for innovation and was able to shuffle them with confidence and vision.

It took a while to gather a group as the hiring team had only a few basic requirements and brief project description to work with. Finally the group was settled in with young guys who for a relatively small scholarship were happy to gain new knowledge and experience working with big projects like this one. At the close of the project, if successful, they were promised to continue employment with the company as regular employees, along with all accompanying benefits. For young mathematicians that looked like an attractive offer. The company prepared a room at the far end of the office corridor. This fact made their project seem a bit mysterious to everyone passing by. But there was no secret. Top management simply kept it low-profile to see what the outcome would be.

Headed by Brian, the group of four started working on modeling and analyzing data. For the mentor, the project was as new as it was for the team. With several crucial knowledge gaps, he required extra time to learn and consider potential blockers. The company invested money in mentors' education time, as the entire project looked nothing similar to what the company did before.

To act like a real tech team, Brian gave them concrete project criteria and deadlines that helped to manage the students, not yet professional enough. After several months of experimenting with large amounts of data and mathematical models, they finally achieved what their mentor had expected. But not everything went smoothly.

During the first month of experiments they took a wrong path that meant they had to start from the middle. On top of this, one team member preferred to work alone. While independence was appreciated early on, it eventually turned into a permanent behaviour. Being silent most of the time, it led to communication issues with the group and mentor. Brian had to overcome these obstacles and move forward as a team.

Anyway, it was time to get ready for the final presentation to the top management.

Being a bit stressy for young talents, it went great. Having a strong sense of connection to something bigger than just models, the young mathematicians proved their contribution to the company's success. And as was promised, several of them joined the company as permanent employees. The project became one of the business development use cases the company utilized for selling their services to end customers, once the boom of data science and data analytics projects emerged.

This group was not the first, who set a foundation for a long-term story with research and development in the company. What started as a small idea and experiment with new technologies brought success and revenue to the company. Later the management decided to grow such initiatives into a bigger department with more people onboard and new challenges to become a business.

For Brian, this was not the last significant project he was part of. As a true pioneer in adopting technologies, he continued working in this role, which I believe is his mission — to make technologies deliver the best for the business and this world.

In an era of progress, tech companies compete for talents to maintain an advantage on the market they operate. Having enough talents at the right time and place is still one of the top priorities of many fast developing businesses. Easy logic. You have enough people, they generate money. Not enough people? It causes money and opportunity losses for the company. To maintain a competitive advantage, companies can set up their own laboratories to grow young talents, explore new recruiting approaches, invest in strategic partnerships, and establish internal resources as pool or bench teams to rapidly react to any market or world trend.

Resource or pool teams are often made of specialists who, at some point of time, lose their allocation on a project for different reasons. It can be a planned event, like a project closure. Or something unexpected, like a budget shortage on the customer's side or a change of priorities in business. During a crisis, companies usually freeze new hires, focusing more on existing personnel to save costs. And then optimizing human capital takes the form of teams' restructuring, retraining and other approaches to enhance efficiency.

Tech companies establish resource teams aiming to influence business profitability through proper resource utilization and skills development. And that made resource teams an important part of any company learning culture.

Here is a story of Martin, who was a technical manager in one of the tech companies I have observed. Working more than four years in this role and feeling somewhat tired of tasks encouraged him to seek a new assignment inside the company.

His super power in people management and emotional intelligence, together with a business mindset, nailed it. He was invited to lead the resource team (also called bench or talent pool), as one of the most unrecognized departments to change the existing utilization process that already required fresh air.

In the company, where every technical working hour has to be billed and contributed to the company revenue, having someone with no active responsibilities and tasks for a long time leads to financial losses. To prevent these cases the company leaders needed someone to drive the team. All to make sure that everyone on the bench brings value, would it be directly tied to revenue or supporting broader company processes and their efficiency.

People in the company rumored, the resource team was associated with uncertainty and an underprivileged position. Being part of the resource team unspokenly added a tag *something is not right with this particular specialist's performance.* Why would they be allocated there when numerous projects suffered from a shortage of resources? Literally, as the new head of the team, Martin needed to reassure everyone of the team's capabilities, dispelling many myths that had taken place.

Who was most often in Martin's team who did come – then went. The team was filled with a diverse mix of personalities:

- Recent graduates from the company internships who were still awaiting their assignments on projects. Usually young, lively and hungry for new skills, they were ready to sprint once the project appeared on a radar.

- So-called low performers, who for different reasons, could not provide enough value to a particular project. In times of a shortage of resources, big tech companies prefer to keep most of these applicants onboard knowing the volatility of their status. In one project, an individual may show less performance due to no fit to the team. But in another project within the same company, they could deliver significant value.

- Rare-skill specialists who were kept in advance for upcoming business challenges. These are individuals who handle knowledge of a unique technology for the company. They could be a solo representative of a particular technology. Or being proficient with technology that is hard to find on the job market.

- Proactive employees who were able to finish their learning earlier than planned and expected new assignments just the next day. These individuals are typically employees who work at a high speed and performance. They aim to leave the temporary team as quickly as possible to join any customer project.

- People who disagreed with their allocation to the resource team. These individuals typically exhibit two behaviors: acceptance and complaining. They either strive to finish their allocation efficiently and start new customer projects. Or express dissatisfaction with their training plans, new managers and various other reasons.

- People who enjoyed learning instead of working on a real project. For different reasons and for some time, these employees prefer learning over working on customers. This often occurs with individuals who possess certain privileges, like a rare skill set or their seniority status. It may be laziness too. But in tech companies, this trick does not work for long and usually ends with a quit from the company.

These are some of the characters who I remember. But definitely not all. Challenging combination, ha?

In big tech companies, resource teams usually team up with various company structures, where sales, engineering, and learning take a crucial part. Martin expected the learning team to collaborate on creating personal development plans, allocating budget for people's retraining if necessary, finding training programs and mentors, and organizing the process of new learning. But things didn't go as he expected. Being far from becoming a substitute of the learning team, Martin wanted them to focus on their shared mission: to grow a culture of high performance. Slowly Martin succeeded in making their communication more productive.

He started with making proper resourcing processes planning, tracking people's performances and aligning budgets to reflect key team metrics. And making sure that all people were going through the interview process to find their next assignment in the company. Along with it, he shared bi-weekly team progress and achievements in one of the company chats. This way he wanted to reassure people in the company:

1.   The resource team is here for far more than keeping unassigned people on the bench.

2.   We are here to maintain a team of motivated employees and provide them with further project opportunities as promptly as they can be managed.

3.   The team spends big, but also wins big in a long-term perspective.

And, it worked well for the team and Martin's visibility and leadership.

Along with minimizing waste and optimizing processes, the company wanted him to support internal projects with automation. Plus, Martin's management finally looked at the resource team as one of the possible solutions to have their own innovative projects.

It can be said, as a head of the team, Martin was functioning in the survival mode. The number of people continuously joining and leaving from and to his team only grew. Projects were on his plate one by one. Having spent several years working in such an intense rhythm, Martin became someone who required optimization and a lifebuoy.

After several rounds of communication, the company decided to split responsibilities between several people to maximize efficiency and manage overload in the resource team. Martin continued driving internal projects and startups, focusing more on revenue generation and business scaling. The time he juggled several projects was filled with success stories of others. It taught Martin adaptability to adjust his management style and creative approach to meet the needs of his employer and resource team applicants.

With all the projects completed, Martin made a significant change in the company's learning culture.

Feeling secure is what individuals and companies strive for. Prior and amidst crisis, companies implement their contingency plans, save cash, optimize their team setups, freeze projects and initiatives to ensure the company's stability and profitability. In a stable and economically growing environment, big efforts are given to investing in new inventions, improvements, and new revenue streams. It is here that research and development labs, resource teams and other organizational structures aim to foster the culture of growth, continuous learning, resilience, and risk-protected environments.

At the same time, for hired employees and individuals, the surviving approach can take the form of adopting new knowledge and skills, building networks of contacts, and looking for prospective opportunities. It works best if both parties' strategies match.

Changes are inevitable.

Learning comes to us on the first day of our life. What starts in the family, when we discover the world with its inhabitants, continues at schools and colleges with tables and grades. Later we begin a new learning chapter in the companies and outside them.

Spending one-third of our lives working, tech people seek meaningful jobs and environments, where they can obtain new competencies, open up new contacts and opportunities. Broad learning cultures together with company leadership support their curiosity and create conditions under which their willingness to learn and share only grows, forcing changes in their lives.

Along with recognition by promotion or salary raise, there are new identities that tech people seek. Each has its own scale of identities or roles they want to fulfill. Tech companies enable their employees with resources and environments to leave their legacy in this world: to be remembered as a good mentor, teacher, manager, team leader, business owner, and inventor. To be remembered for the insights they left in their articles, books, software applications and documented discoveries for next generations.

Tech companies with strong learning cultures and diverse mindsets can turn into a workspace where employees explore and connect with their life missions. It is important for many tech people to stay social and help others understand their paths and follow their careers or life dreams. They volunteer to become speakers and mentors to positively impact the society and add more sense to their daily routine. They want to be among other open-minded people and thus, they join different clubs, communities and thematic events.

When tech people are bored in their jobs, they creatively escape sameness by looking around for new projects and technologies. Because no matter the age, people want to play and have fun. Techies actively search for any kind of entertainment in work routines, would it be a gamified learning or event like hackathons.

Sometimes, however, they sabotage bringing a change into their lives, as they are afraid of success and transformations coming to them with learning. This sabotage can go away someday with a new confidence growing inside. Or it will bring them another road they will be eager to turn.

The process of learning in IT works both alone and in groups, as people grow through personal effort and by discussing ideas with others. There is always so much to learn and do, so it is easy to be overwhelmed with all the things. In this case, learning from people's successes and failures becomes a necessary resource. The latter prepares tech people for uncertainties. By inviting partners and customers to learn from each other, a company creates a collective intelligence in different forms. They know how beneficial it is for the business to have valuable knowledge communicated and artifacts stored on the company shared platform.

Tech people cultivate a learning culture within themselves as they know that this world is not a stable place. To adapt to any crises, they look around to make themselves stronger and more skillful than before with the help of new learning. On the company level, this preparation could be seen in different organizational structures, like research and development labs or resource teams. When everything changes so fast, these structures and people experimenting there with new technologies and approaches, become value and revenue-generating machines. At the same time, they fulfill the needs of employees seeking new challenges and inspirations.

Being in a position to influence company processes means you have a possibility to check up your learning culture and create an environment where people can grow exponentially and bring a significant value to the company.

As someone who undertakes any learning, remind yourself of the reasons that brought you there – whether it is a new set of skills you need for your project or a career promotion. Question yourself more and look beyond the answer to see what truly stands behind this learning need. Maybe you will find that all you learn now, leads you towards your dream or a big roadmap you aim to discover.

1. Page 6. Jack Walsh Quote
   https://www.oreilly.com/library/view/the-little-book/9781292148458/html/chapter-035.html

2. Page 9. Edward T. Hall Understanding the culture of a company
   https://laconteconsulting.com/2018/04/12/understanding-the-culture-part-1-surface/

3. Page 12. Git (a distributed version control system)
   https://en.wikipedia.org/wiki/Git

4. Page 14. 360 degree feedback model
   https://en.wikipedia.org/wiki/360-degree_feedback

5. Page 20. Nelson Mandela Quote
   https://www.nelsonmandela.org/nm100-education

6. Page 29. Todd Kashdan Curiosiy
   https://toddkashdan.com/curiosity/

7. Page 57. Westworld series by HBO company
   https://www.hbo.com/westworld

8. Page 75. Hackathon definition
   https://en.wikipedia.org/wiki/Hackathon

9. Page 103. Darwin's Quote. Megginson, 'Lessons from Europe for American Business', Southwestern Social Science Quarterly (1963) 44(1): 3-13, at p. 4.